D1433607

Best of British
COOKBOOK

MARKS & SPENCER

Best of British COOKBOOK

Pamela Gwyther

Marks and Spencer p.l.c.
PO Box 3339
Chester CH99 9QS

www.marksandspencer.com

ISBN: 1-84461-152-3

Printed in Dubai

Produced by the Bridgewater Book Company Ltd.

Photographer: Laurie Evans
Home Economist: Annie Rigg
Location Photography: Caroline Jones

NOTES FOR THE READER

- This book uses both metric and imperial measurements. Follow the same units of measurement throughout; do not mix metric and imperial.
- All spoon measurements are level: teaspoons are assumed to be 5 ml, and tablespoons are assumed to be 15 ml.
- Unless otherwise stated, milk is assumed to be full fat, eggs and individual vegetables such as potatoes are medium, and pepper is freshly ground black pepper.
- Recipes using raw or very lightly cooked eggs should be avoided by infants, the elderly, pregnant women, convalescents and anyone suffering from an illness.
- The times given are an approximate guide only. Preparation times differ according to the techniques used by different people and the cooking times may also vary from those given.

CONTENTS

INTRODUCTION

'Best of British?' Nowadays this can mean a bowl of pasta, a chicken curry or a stir-fry, but many of our favourite foods are still the classic British recipes of our childhood. Some may take a little time to prepare, but there is nothing to beat the joy of going to a dinner with friends and being served pork with crackling and apple sauce, or of waking up to a full English breakfast, or even just snuggling up on a winter's night with a helping of steamed syrup pudding and real custard.

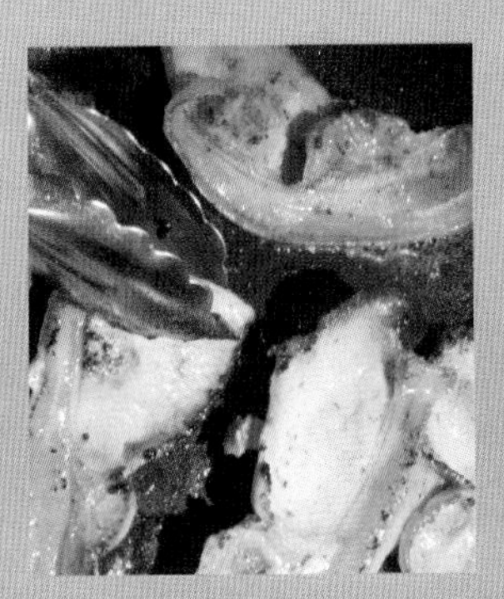

Many of life's happiest moments are forever entwined with the cooking of our mothers and grandmothers. Sunday lunch is still a ritual that many families like to keep, perhaps the only meal when they sit down together and discuss their week. As a child, my Sunday roast was usually at my grandparents' house, when the treat was to have a glass of orange squash to drink. It was very traditional; the meal included a roast meat (usually beef), Yorkshire pudding (lots of it, even if the joint wasn't beef), roast potatoes and a couple of vegetables. A pudding was also confined to Sundays (although we might have an occasional rice pudding in the week) and was usually an apple or other fruit pie made in a deep dish with shortcrust pastry on top and sprinkled with sugar. Grandfather carved the joint and we all had to watch and admire his proficiency, just as we had to congratulate grandmother on her beautifully cooked meat. The Yorkshire pudding, vegetables and gravy were usually served onto our plates and we were expected to eat every scrap – wasting food was not allowed.

Before the advent of ready-prepared suppers and today's incredible choice of produce, evening meals tended to be quite simple. For me it was sausages or cheese on toast, perhaps a bacon and egg pie and a piece of fruit for 'sweet'. When we arrived home from school there was often some home-made fruit cake or biscuits, which we ate with a glass of milk. In the holidays, there was time to help make the cakes, particularly Eccles cakes shaped from my mother's leftover pastry scraps. I will always remember the warmth and delicious smells of the big kitchen and the magic of simple ingredients being turned into delicious dishes and meals. I was encouraged to help with the basic preparations and shelling peas, trimming sprouts, mixing batter and making crumble for puddings were all part of my British culinary upbringing.

I am also one of those people who loved school dinners. I say 'I loved them', but there were certainly one or two things I couldn't manage, especially our lamb stew and 'cow heel pie' – I know Desperate Dan is supposed to have lived on it, but not me! Shepherd's pie, cottage pie, stew and dumplings were all wonderful. Like many other children, I dreaded the cabbage days, which you could smell from up the road, but carrots and mashed potatoes were brilliant. Puddings were even better and I adored jam roly-poly (sometimes served with a 'pink' custard sauce), treacle tart and chocolate sponge with chocolate sauce. I even liked prunes and custard! We would arrange our stones around the edges of the plate while we chanted 'Tinker, tailor, soldier, sailor, rich man, poor man, beggar man, thief' and then argue the outcome.

CELEBRATING WITH BRITISH FOOD

British food comes into its own at celebrations – times when we treasure making dishes properly, in the traditional way. For many people, Christmas just isn't Christmas without exactly the same food they feasted on as children, right down to the crunchiness of the potatoes or the thickness of the gravy. All the planning and preparation beforehand is as important as the day itself, starting with making the mincemeat, then the pudding and the cake, and finally the icing.

Christmas Eve in Britain has never been the celebration of food that it is in Europe, but many families have their own rituals. My family all used to go to church at midnight, then after church we would have a supper of meat pie and pickled red cabbage, which was very welcome after walking home through the cold night. Before hanging up our empty stockings by the fireplace, we left out a glass of sherry for Father Christmas and a couple of mince pies for the reindeer.

Christmas Day began with the opening of stockings and eating the oranges and chocolates usually found in them. The meal preparations would have to run like clockwork. Someone, usually my grandmother, would get up very early to put the turkey in the oven. Later, we were all roped in to help prepare the vegetables

and to lay the table with crackers and candles. Then we would go to church before returning home to open our presents.

Christmas lunch was always turkey, roast potatoes, sprouts, carrots and stuffing, usually sage and onion. The gravy was made with flour and coloured using gravy browning. Pudding was traditional and very heavy, made with suet and flour with all the fruit we use today, though now I make a 'healthy' version with wholemeal breadcrumbs, but without suet or added sugar. I also remember we had white sauce flavoured with brandy or rum, whereas now we always have brandy butter. Mince pies were served with a little Lancashire cheese, but I can't ever remember having any room for them. We always had to finish lunch in time for the Queen's broadcast and we sat and listened in silence. Afterwards, we all had to help wash up (no dishwasher). Later in the afternoon we would visit my aunt and her family and have yet more food – tea with sandwiches, trifle and Christmas cake. After all that, Boxing Day was luckily always considered a day of rest and we were able to stay in bed and relax. The meal that day was usually ham or gammon served simply with jacket potatoes, leftover vegetables and home-made chutney and pickles.

No other day comes close to Christmas in food terms, but Easter in our house always had to include a chocolate Easter egg hunt. While Easter lunch was not quite so set as Christmas, we usually had roast Welsh lamb with roast potatoes and roast parsnips, always leeks and sometimes even laver bread if we could find it – a proper Welsh Easter. There is no traditional pudding for Easter, but simnel cake is Easter's delicious equivalent of Christmas cake.

Other days associated with food in the British calendar include Mothering Sunday (the fourth Sunday in Lent), when historically apprentices were allowed home to visit their families and take a simnel cake as a present. Pancake Day and Bonfire Night are eating opportunities, the latter with food eaten around the bonfire: jacket potatoes cooked in the fire, sausage rolls, hot soup, gingerbread and Parkin are all traditional warmers. St David's Day can be celebrated with a traditional Welsh meal of laver bread followed by fresh salmon, then Snowdon pudding and Caerphilly cheese. St George's Day, sadly, is rarely marked with traditional English food, but Burns' Night is another occasion to celebrate – try haggis followed by venison casserole, neeps and tatties and a dessert of Atholl Brose.

Birthdays will always be associated with special party food – crisps, baby sausages, sandwiches, jelly, ice cream and, of course, the cake. Anniversaries are also important in the food diary. Rather than going out to eat I usually prepare something delicious in the comfort of our home. Lobster, scallops, monkfish or a Scottish fillet steak usually feature, followed by simple strawberries and cream or a syllabub – ideal for two people.

BRITISH FOOD ON HOLIDAY

Seaside holidays at home are a uniquely British food experience – day trips to Blackpool with aunts and uncles and cousins; candy floss, toffee apples and hot dogs at the fun fair; 'Kiss me Quick' hats and Blackpool rock with the writing going right through the middle; picnicking on the beach with a primus stove to heat the water for tea; playing games and eating very sandy sandwiches and cake; jellied eels and cockles, potted shrimps and fish and chips before the journey home. 'Mad dogs and Englishmen go out in the midday sun' – and the wind and the rain! We had picnics regardless of our inclement climate, we ignored the elements and sat dripping, freezing and windswept on a beach whatever the weather.

Holidays away from the seashore can be food treats too. In Scotland, I've eaten porridge, Arbroath smokies, Aberdeen Angus beef, venison, shortbread and berries, and learnt to appreciate malt whisky. Welsh holidays always include cockles, laver bread, salmon, lamb, leeks and bara brith, while in Cornwall, oysters, crab, clotted cream teas and pasties are among the memorable things to eat.

During the summer months, all those great British occasions in the social calendar seem to feature food in some form or other. The Henley Regatta is all about watching the rowing while picnicking by the river or in a boat with a hamper containing delicious goodies. Eating strawberries and cream at Wimbledon during the tennis fortnight is a treat not to be missed, while a picnic taken in the car park from the boot of the car at the races on Derby Day or at Royal Ascot is a British institution. The experience of opera at Glyndebourne is enhanced by smoked salmon, beef Wellington, salads, and strawberries or raspberries and cream during the interval. And, if you are lucky enough to be invited, tea at a Royal Garden Party at Buckingham Palace features food served in miniature portions, most beautifully presented.

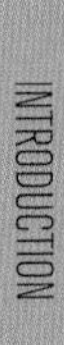
INTRODUCTION

WHAT IS BRITISH FOOD?

There has traditionally been a rich cornucopia of edible materials in Britain: Scottish beef, Welsh lamb, English pork, bacon and ham, and fresh fish from ports all around the coast, where British trawlermen go out in all weathers to bring us their fresh catch. There are countless varieties of potatoes, and seasonal vegetables vary from peas and beans in the summer to leeks and sprouts in the winter. Fruit include apples and pears in the autumn and soft fruits like strawberries and raspberries in summer.

There is also a rich heritage of delicious local specialities. I've mentioned some from Devon and Cornwall, Wales and Scotland, but there are many others. In the north of England, both Lancashire and Yorkshire have good reputations for cheeses. Somerset is known for its apples and cider (and Cheddar cheese) and Wiltshire for its dairy farming, lamb and bacon, while Kent, 'the garden of England', produces apples, hops for beer and now grapes for wine. In East Anglia, Colchester is famous for its oysters and seafood, Lowestoft and Great Yarmouth for their fish, and the region produces much of our butter and milk, turkeys, ducklings and pigs. Lincolnshire, a very flat county, is where many of our vegetables are grown, especially potatoes, peas, beans, lettuces and cucumbers. The Midlands region produces many cheeses, particularly Stilton – the king of cheeses – Leicester, Red Leicester and Sage Derby. Gloucestershire produces Double Gloucester cheese and the finest pork and bacon, while Worcestershire has given its name to a piquant sauce that is used widely in cooking.

Our wet climate and our geographical situation as a cold northern area tempered by the warm Gulf Stream are the main factors behind the food we eat. They particularly encourage the production of cereals (wheat for bread, cakes

and pies and oats for porridge), grass (to raise cattle for dairy products and beef) and fruit and vegetables. Our island coastline means that we have access to an abundance of fish in the waters that surround us.

The climate also created the need for our preserving techniques. In the past, winter meant there was little meat and few vegetables so, when they were in abundance during the summer and autumn months, the housewife would preserve them. This could be by either smoking and salting meat and fish or by pickling and salting vegetables before storing them in jars. Fruit was also bottled and made into jams, jellies and chutneys. Of course, this was before the invention of the freezer to preserve meat, fish, fruit and vegetables.

Foreign influences from other countries have been absorbed over the centuries and brought us new foods and ingredients, and also new cooking techniques and styles. The Romans introduced pheasant, guinea fowl, deer, figs, walnuts, chestnuts, cabbage, turnips and many herbs. The Saxons and Angles brought dairy produce and the Normans contributed fruit and different cereal products. Sugar came to Britain with the returning Crusaders. Sixteenth-century explorers found the New World and with it turkeys, tomatoes, peppers, chillies, vanilla and potatoes, which, of course, became a staple in Britain and Ireland. Our other colonies gave us spices and curries from India, butter and cheese from New Zealand, and fascinating recipes from Africa and Asia. European influences came to bear when people did their 'grand tour of Europe' and visited all the capitals, bringing back new ideas. More recently, we have been influenced by the Pacific rim countries and their foods, from Thai and Japanese to Australian. In fact, our modern British food is a fusion of world cuisines and produce.

HEALTHY BRITISH FOOD

Because most of us now lead a relatively sedentary lifestyle, we have to take care in our choice of food. In the past, labour on the land was intensive and men and women had to eat large meals to fuel their work. As the industrial revolution got underway, there was less heavy work and meals needed to be adjusted to the decreased workload, meaning less fat and more vegetables. However, today too many of us are not only overweight, but obese. So we need to choose foods that are lighter and do not contain as much fat or highly refined carbohydrates.

Breakfasts should be satisfying and quick to eat. Cereal, toast and orange juice are often preferred in the week. The cereal should be wholegrain and the toast wholemeal because these are complex carbohydrates and take longer to be digested. This stops you from feeling hungry for longer. At the weekend, a cooked breakfast is often the preferred option, either eggs cooked in some way and grilled bacon or, occasionally, the 'full monty', as described in Chapter 1.

Soups can be just vegetables and stock, cooked and liquidized with no additions. In times past, the soups would be thickened with white flour and perhaps enriched with egg yolks and cream, but this is unnecessary if good fresh vegetables are used which provide all the flavour and enjoyment.

White fish has always been a healthy option due to its lack of fat. Oily fish contains healthy omega-3 oils. Fish was once seen as a cheap food, but is now relatively expensive so we need to educate ourselves to pay more for the fish we buy. It is strange that we don't mind paying for expensive cuts of meat like steaks, but are reluctant to pay similar prices for fish.

Red meat is generally viewed as relatively unhealthy owing to its fat content and its contribution to high cholesterol levels, and hence heart disease. However, we don't need to eat red meat every day, so when we do we should choose our cut carefully, cooking it in the best possible way to ensure tenderness and good flavours. Poultry and game are a healthier meat option, although duck and goose need careful cooking and the excess fat removed before serving. The reduced use of sauces in recipes today is a benefit to our health and means we eat proteins simply and enjoy their natural flavours rather than swamp them in rich sauces.

Puddings and desserts are a part of our diet where many of us might find room for improvement. There are many pre-prepared

puddings available that contain too much fat and sugar, which we know is very bad for us. The answer is to make your own puddings and desserts so that you know exactly what goes into them, and to keep puddings as treats for weekends and special occasions. During the week, fresh fruit and natural yogurt are the best choices if you need something sweet to round off a meal.

Tea-time treats should be exactly as the name suggests: 'treats', not to be eaten every day but enjoyed occasionally. Home-made cakes and biscuits are delicious and you can make them from the best ingredients, but their intake should be limited.

We now stand at a crossroads in British eating. On the one side, we have the rich heritage of traditional British foods, developed and influenced over the years by our climate and location, and by our history. At their finest these foods offer a wide range of delicious, healthy flavoursome dishes. On the other side, we have cheap foodstuffs, produced to meet the needs of an increasingly pressured society, but perhaps not as wholesome as the traditional alternatives. This book celebrates these traditions, materials and recipes. I hope you will be inspired to return to, or to try for yourself, these old favourites and celebrate with me 'The Best of British'.

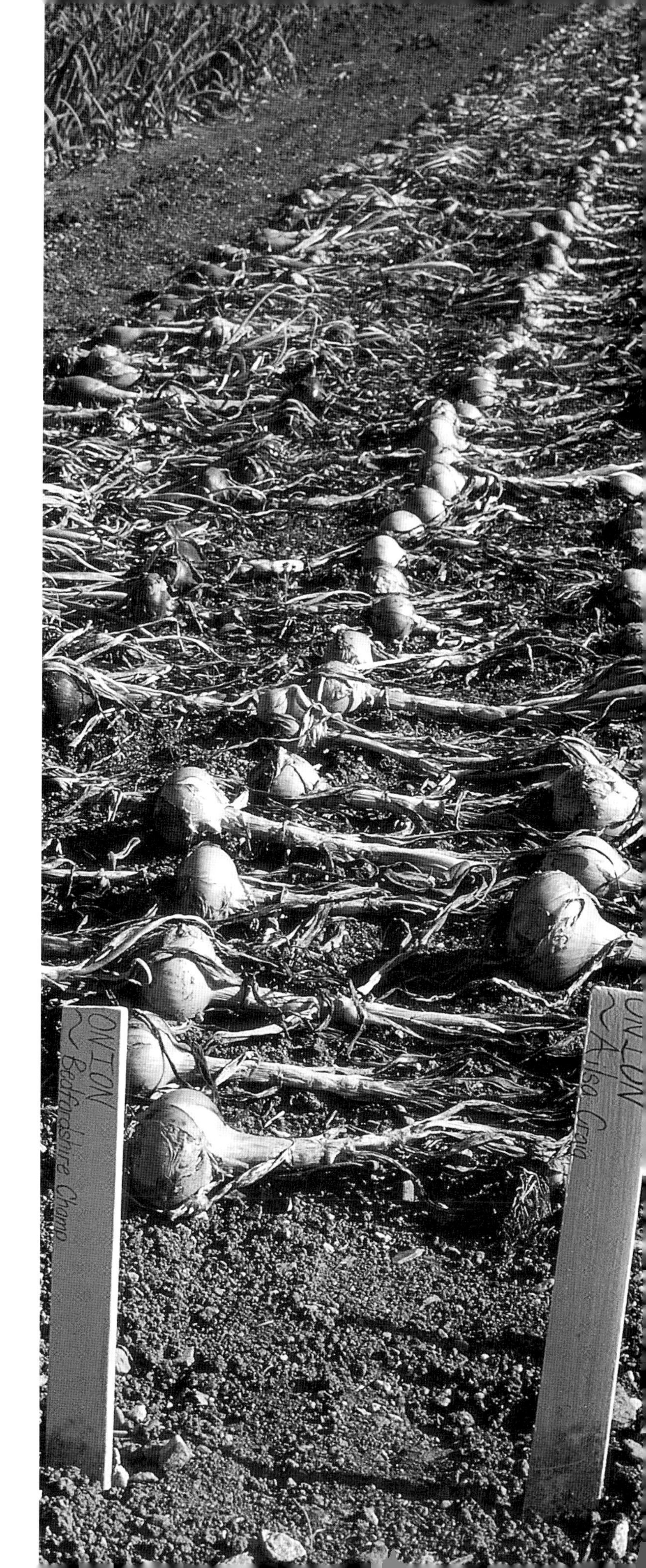

1 BRITISH BREAKFASTS

Breakfast gets its name from 'breaking the fast', the meal that starts the day, after fasting through the night. Early man woke with the sun, not an alarm clock, and would have eaten anything that he had managed to find or hunt the day before. It would have been a limited meal, and only as he began to cultivate the land would he have had a wider choice. Throughout time, the type of breakfast eaten depended on lifestyle. Labourers might have had a large breakfast, but the non-working classes would have had a drink and perhaps some light food. By the late nineteenth century, breakfast had evolved into a more formal meal for some. Taken in the dining room and consisting of many courses, both hot and cold, breakfast was served as a buffet where guests could help themselves. This is the origin of the 'Great British Breakfast', with sideboards groaning under a variety of dishes.

By the twentieth century, many people had begun to go out for the full British breakfast. The British Rail version became very well known, and commuters took advantage of the service. 'Greasy spoon' cafés suddenly appeared everywhere, on high streets, at railway stations, motorway service stations and roadside catering vans, all providing a full English breakfast. Those who had to stay away in hotels and guest houses were always able to eat bacon and eggs in some form, and often could order up 'the full monty' – bacon, eggs, sausages, mushrooms, fried bread and tomatoes – washed down with a good cup of strong tea.

Breakfast has always been popular on holiday too. Many establishments serve an 'all-day breakfast', and with visitors getting up at all times of the day and wanting a quick, hot, filling meal, what better than a huge plate of bacon and eggs with all the trimmings? It has even spread to foreign resorts like the Costa Brava and Ibiza, often connected with absorbing the previous night's intake of cheap plonk!

Today, the habit of sitting down to breakfast during the week, particularly as a family, has begun to disappear. Many women go out to work and people leave the house at different times, often without eating anything at all. This is not a good habit. We need a healthy breakfast so that we have enough energy, both physical and mental, to concentrate at work or school. Schoolchildren can now be seen outside sweetshops or at the railway station buying crisps and chocolate before going to school, which is hardly the best start to the day. It is for this reason that the Government is thinking of starting school earlier and providing breakfast to ensure pupils have something nourishing in their bodies to help them concentrate throughout the morning.

If we do eat breakfast at home it is often cereal based which, if served with skimmed milk and without too much sugar, can be a good way to start the day. The habit of drinking fruit juices is increasing, as is the more modern intake of 'smoothies', which are a good way to enjoy some of the recommended daily amount of fruit.

Luckily at weekends, when there is time, we can still indulge in a good old proper British breakfast. Couples may choose to eat theirs in bed; kids like to breakfast in front of the TV; and singles may get together with friends, either at home or at their local breakfast place. Smoked fish and kedgeree may also be served, particularly when entertaining or when friends stay for the weekend. A big breakfast means the cook can have a leisurely start and make one meal instead of two: 'brunch', breakfast and lunch combined.

This is surely the best-known British dish of all! If we are to 'eat breakfast like a king, lunch like a gentleman and supper like a pauper', then this is the meal to kick-start the day. For most people, however, a 'full English' every day is too much, so this is a dish best prepared at the weekend after a night out and with plenty of time to cook and enjoy it. Personally, I prefer my English breakfast as brunch, with all morning – and all afternoon if I want – to eat and read the papers.

FULL ENGLISH BREAKFAST

Serves 1

2 good-quality pork sausages

2–3 smoked back bacon rashers

2 eggs

1 slice 2-day-old wholemeal bread (optional)

1 large tomato, halved

vegetable oil, to drizzle

salt and pepper

2–3 mushrooms

1 Place the sausages under a hot grill and grill for about 15–20 minutes, turning frequently, until they are well browned.

2 Meanwhile, place the bacon rashers in a dry frying pan and fry for 2–4 minutes on each side, depending on how crisp you like your bacon. Remove from the frying pan, leaving all the excess bacon fat, and keep the bacon warm. The frying pan can then be used to fry the eggs if you choose to have them fried. See page 28: Ways with Eggs.

3 Alternatively, use the delicious bacon fat to make fried bread. Heat the frying pan and place the bread in the fat. Cook for 1–2 minutes on one side, then turn over and repeat. Do not cook too quickly or the bread will burn.

4 The tomato halves can be placed under the hot grill with the sausages. Drizzle with a little oil and season to taste with salt and pepper before grilling for 3–4 minutes.

5 The mushrooms can be grilled with the tomatoes or quickly fried in the frying pan with a little extra oil added.

6 Arrange the sausages, bacon, eggs, fried bread, tomatoes and mushrooms on a large hot platter and serve at once.

ACCOMPANIMENTS

A 'full' breakfast sometimes includes black or white pudding and often includes baked beans. To complete the breakfast, freshly made toast served with butter and marmalade is traditional.

Whether it is a quick breakfast to get you fuelled up in the morning or a late-night snack to help absorb the evening's alcohol, a bacon buttie certainly takes a lot of beating. It may not be the most fancy food, but the bacon buttie arouses some strong opinions. Should the bread be grilled or fried? White or wholemeal? To sauce or not to sauce? The only general consensus seems to be that the bread must be thick and it must be spread with a lot of butter. With no definitive recipe, adapt the outline below as you see fit.

BACON BUTTIES

Serves 1

2 smoked bacon rashers

15 g/½ oz butter, softened

2 slices thick white or brown bread

pepper

1 tomato, sliced (optional)

sauce of choice (brown sauce, tomato ketchup or mustard)

1 Cut the rashers of bacon in half so that you have 2 pieces of back bacon and 2 pieces of streaky.

2 Place the bacon under a hot grill and grill, turning frequently, until the bacon is cooked and as crispy as you like it.

3 Meanwhile, butter the bread.

4 Place 2 pieces of bacon on one slice of bread and season with a grinding of pepper. Add the tomato, if using, and the sauce. Top with the remaining bacon and the other slice of bread and eat immediately.

VARIATIONS

Toasted Sarnies

Make as above but toast the bread on both sides either under a medium grill or in a toaster before making the sandwich.

After a Late Night

After a late night out, there is nothing like a fry-up sandwich to settle the stomach and fill the hunger gap. Fry bacon and sausages together in a frying pan until they are cooked. You might take the bacon out and keep warm, allowing the sausages to cook for longer. Fry bread on one side only, then spread with the sauce of your choice. Pile on the bacon with cut-up sausages, top with more fried bread and eat immediately while still hot.

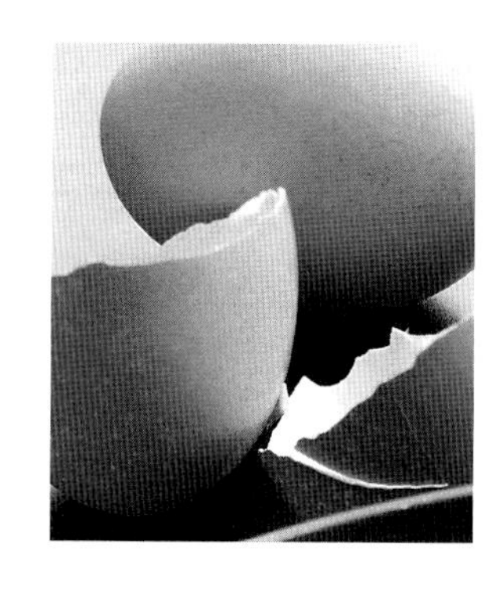

Eggs are for many people the number one comfort food, and if your happiest childhood memories include boiled eggs and soldiers, you're probably one of them. Eggs are very quick to prepare, nutritious, and can be cooked in so many different ways, from boiling and frying to scrambling, poaching and baking, that you don't have to keep them just for breakfast. A really fresh omelette cooked with a handful of fresh herbs or a filling makes one of the most elegant of all light lunch or supper dishes.

WAYS WITH EGGS

BOILING

You will need a saucepan large enough to cook the number of eggs required, but not so large that the eggs can move around too freely and crack. It is a good idea to have the eggs at room temperature to prevent cracking. Bring the water to a gentle simmer and lower the eggs in using a long-handled spoon. Simmer for 3–4 minutes for soft-boiled, 5–6 for medium-boiled and 10 minutes for hard-boiled. If you are serving hard-boiled eggs cold, always run them under cold water immediately after they are cooked to prevent a black line forming around the yolk.

FRYING

The best way to fry an egg is to fry it in the same frying pan in which you have just fried some bacon. This way you have the delicious bacon fat to baste your egg with. Otherwise, take 1 tablespoon oil or 15 g/½ oz butter and heat in a small frying pan over a medium heat. Break the egg into the frying pan (if you are a beginner it might be wise to break the egg into a cup or ramekin first). Fry for a few seconds until the white sets, then baste with the fat to make sure it is evenly cooked with the white completely set and the yolk still remaining soft in the centre. Remove the egg from the pan using a wooden spatula and allow it to rest on a piece of kitchen paper for a second to absorb any excess fat. Serve immediately.

POACHING

You need a small shallow pan (a small frying pan is ideal) and really fresh eggs for this method. Heat enough water to cover the eggs and break 1 egg into a cup. When the water is at a gentle simmer, carefully pour in the egg and allow the white to coagulate around the yolk. You can now add a further egg (I think 2 cooked together are enough to handle). Poach for 2–3 minutes if you like a soft yolk or for 4–5 minutes for a firmer egg. Remove from the pan using a slotted spoon, drain quickly on kitchen paper and serve immediately.

SCRAMBLING

Allow 2 eggs per person and beat them gently in a basin with a little salt and pepper. Melt 15 g/½ oz butter in a saucepan over a low heat, pour in the beaten eggs and stir gently using a wooden spoon. The egg will start to set on the base of the pan, so lift it away from the base until all the egg is starting to look creamy. Remove from the heat and continue to stir until it does not look wet any more. Serve quickly as you do not want to have rubbery scrambled egg.

BAKING

If you have a large number of people to feed, baked eggs are a simple and delicious way to serve them. Generously butter a number of small ramekins and break 1 egg into each dish. Season well with salt and pepper and spoon over 1 tablespoon single cream. Place the dishes in a roasting tin with enough hot water to come halfway up the sides of the dishes and bake at 190°C/375°F/Gas Mark 5 for 15 minutes for a soft egg and 18–20 minutes for a firmer egg.

North of the border porridge is taken seriously, and is still made in the traditional Scottish way – the oats cooked in water and stirred with a 'spurtle' stick. Although porridge oats are often used to make the more modern muesli, there is nothing like a bowl of the real thing to set you up on a cold day. And you don't have to be a purist – a puddle of cream, sprinkling of dark brown sugar or drizzle of golden honey can turn this healthy, quick-to-prepare food into something irresistible.

PORRIDGE

Serves 1

300 ml/10 fl oz water

40 g/1½ oz coarse oats

salt

1 Heat the water in a saucepan until boiling and pour in the oats, stirring continuously.

2 Allow to return to the boil and continue to stir for 2–3 minutes (or according to the packet instructions).

3 Add salt to taste and serve at once in a warm bowl.

ACCOMPANIMENTS

In Scotland, porridge is traditionally served very simply as above, but in England people normally prefer their porridge to be sweet. Serve with muscovado sugar, honey or golden syrup. The addition of milk is also more usual south of the border – you can make the porridge using all milk or half milk and half water, and serve with a helping of pouring cream on top. Some people like a grating of nutmeg, or a 'wee dram' can be poured over for a special occasion like New Year's Day. For a delicious and healthy option, serve your porridge with some fresh fruit, such as peaches or blueberries.

PUB

This Anglo-Indian dish of curried rice and fish was brought back to Britain in the time of the Raj by those who had developed a love of curry in their years abroad and couldn't wait to spice up the bland food of home. It was traditionally served as part of a breakfast buffet so that guests could help themselves from the sideboard, and today it makes a good dish to serve at brunch. Invite some friends over to chat and read the papers and serve Buck's Fizz to make the party really sparkle.

KEDGEREE

Serves 4

450 g/1 lb undyed smoked haddock, skinned

2 tbsp olive oil

1 onion, finely chopped

1 tsp mild curry paste

175 g/6 oz long-grain rice

salt and pepper

55 g/2 oz butter

3 hard-boiled eggs

2 tbsp chopped fresh parsley, to garnish

1 Place the fish in a large saucepan and cover with water. Bring the water to the boil, then turn down to a simmer and poach the fish for 8–10 minutes until it flakes easily.

2 Remove the fish and keep warm, reserving the water in a jug or bowl.

3 Add the oil to the saucepan and gently soften the onion for about 4 minutes. Stir in the curry paste and add the rice.

4 Measure 600 ml/1 pint of the haddock water and return to the saucepan. Bring to a simmer and cover. Cook for 10–12 minutes until the rice is tender and the water has been absorbed. Season to taste with salt and pepper.

5 Flake the fish and add to the saucepan with the butter. Stir very gently over a low heat until the butter has melted. Chop 2 of the hard-boiled eggs and add to the saucepan.

6 Turn the kedgeree into a serving dish, slice the remaining egg and use to garnish. Scatter the parsley over and serve at once.

VARIATION

Kedgeree can also be made with salmon and served as a lunch or supper dish.

Kippers are herrings that have been split open, soaked in brine and then smoked over oak chips. They have a strong smoky flavour and can be quite salty, but make a delicious breakfast. The favoured food of the old-fashioned seaside hotel, kippers come from Scotland and The Isle of Man, which is where I remember having my first kipper on holiday as a child. Kippers can be grilled, fried, jugged or poached, but poaching has the advantage of keeping the fish moist and it also reduces the kipper smell during cooking.

KIPPERS

Serves 1

1 kipper

knob of butter

pepper

to serve

brown bread slices, buttered

lemon wedges

POACHING

1 Place the kipper in a frying pan and cover with water.

2 Bring to the boil, then reduce the heat, cover and simmer gently for about 5 minutes.

3 Drain on kitchen paper and place on a warm plate with a knob of butter on top and some pepper to taste.

4 Serve immediately with the buttered brown bread and a squeeze of lemon juice.

JUGGING

1 Place the kipper in a large earthenware jug.

2 Top up the jug with boiling water and leave to stand for 10 minutes.

3 Drain on kitchen paper and serve immediately as above.

VARIATIONS

Kippers are delicious served with a poached egg on top. They also make a delicious pâté, blended with softened butter and lemon juice.

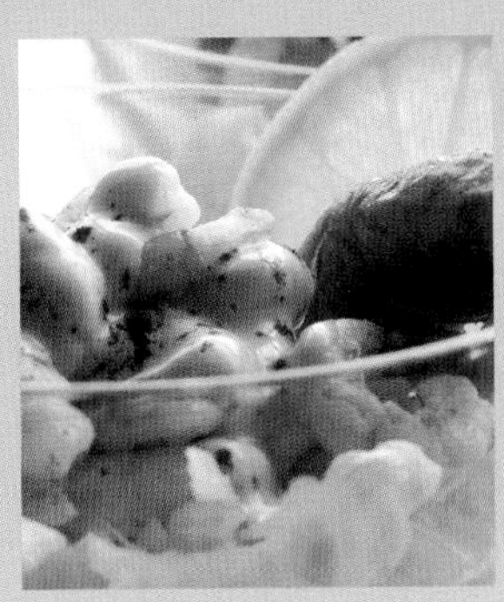

2

SOUPS & STARTERS

Soups have been a staple of British food throughout history. Originally known as a 'pottage', we can even read about it in the Old Testament. Pottage was the dish of the day for working people, and many generations relied on soups to get them through their week. Often soups consisted just of water and anything that could be found to flavour it, such as leaves, herbs, perhaps a little meat or ham and bacon bones. Richer people would have more protein in their soups. Some cereals might be added, or some pulses such as beans. Later, anything growing in the garden by the kitchen door would be used. Meat, poultry, game, fish and shellfish eventually became more common and the types and varieties of soup expanded. Some early recipes have stayed in the British repertoire, but others have been lost over time. Starters are a relatively modern course in a meal and can be vegetable-, fruit-, meat- or fish-based. Whatever you serve, keep your portions small, so that you don't spoil the appetite for what is to follow.

In the eighteenth century, as explorers discovered new foods from around the world, soups started to become more adventurous, such as turtle soup made out of turtles brought from the West Indies. There was also a soup called 'London particular', which was a thick soup named after the London fog. 'Benevolent soup' was so named because it was prepared in soup kitchens and served to the poor.

Beef tea (like a simple beef consommé) was given to the sick and convalescents because it was concentrated protein, which was easy to digest. Chicken soup, as made by Jewish mothers, is still known as 'Jewish penicillin' and is a good cure for all ills. Another memorable soup is Brown Windsor, which was served in second-rate hotels (like Fawlty Towers), consisting of little more than water and a stock cube and, thankfully, is not around any more. Another, tinned tomato soup, has stood the test of time. Although nothing like a home-made tomato soup, it has the comfort factor. Many of us will remember eating it at home when recovering from a cold or flu and appreciating its soothing qualities.

Today, soup is served as the first course of a meal or as a main meal in itself, when it can contain meat or fish and vegetables together with potatoes or beans. A hunk of good bread is all that is needed to complete the meal. Soups may be prepared according to seasons when vegetables are at their best, and can be served cold in the summer months. Vegetable soups can be chunky, like minestrone, or served as a purée, with or without the addition of cream. A suitable garnish is a great final touch. Chopped fresh herbs, croûtons (fried small cubes of bread to give added texture) and swirls of sour cream are all possibilities.

Elaborate starters are often special occasion or restaurant fare, but a starter can consist of a single serving of perhaps just one vegetable. Asparagus, for instance, served hot or cold, is a delicious and simple treat at the beginning of the growing season. Sometimes fruit is served: half an avocado, accompanied by prawns, was a particular favourite during the 1970s, as was grilled grapefruit. Today, fruit starters might include mango or watermelon. Salads, whether simple or a composition of six to eight ingredients tossed together with a fresh dressing, are another good choice of starter. Potted meats and fish have retained their popularity, as have smooth mousses and pâtés, which can be made from sardines, prawns, smoked trout or chicken livers. Quickly made and served in ramekin dishes, these are a traditional choice at dinner parties.

A selection of small starters served before the meal is known as 'hors d'œuvres'. This was a real feature of the 1960s when most restaurants had an hors d'œuvre trolley. More than any other course, starters tend to be fashionable and to change frequently.

Scotch broth is a very nourishing, hearty winter soup that is actually a meal in itself as it contains lamb, lots of vegetables and pearl barley. This is one of those 'one-pot' dishes that used to be served as a soup when people did more manual work, but today it is probably better served as a main course, unless of course you happen to be a farmer or a mountain climber. Because lamb is quite a fatty meat, it is a good idea to make this soup the day before it is needed so that you can cool it and remove any excess fat.

SCOTCH BROTH

Serves 6–8

700 g/1 lb 9 oz neck of lamb

1.7 litres/3 pints water

55 g/2 oz pearl barley

2 onions, chopped

1 garlic clove, finely chopped

3 small turnips, cut into small dice

3 carrots, peeled and finely sliced

2 celery sticks, sliced

2 leeks, sliced

salt and pepper

2 tbsp chopped fresh parsley, to garnish

1 Cut the meat into small pieces, removing as much fat as possible. Put into a large saucepan and cover with the water. Bring to the boil over a medium heat and skim off any scum that appears.

2 Add the pearl barley, reduce the heat and cook gently, covered, for 1 hour.

3 Add the prepared vegetables and season well with salt and pepper. Continue to cook for a further hour. Remove from the heat and allow to cool slightly.

4 Remove the meat from the saucepan using a slotted spoon and strip the meat from the bones. Discard the bones and any fat or gristle. Place the meat back in the saucepan and leave to cool thoroughly, then refrigerate overnight.

5 Scrape the solidified fat off the surface of the soup. Reheat, season with salt and pepper to taste and serve piping hot, garnished with the parsley scattered over the top.

Leeks and potatoes are two of the staple vegetables of Britain and leeks are particularly associated with Wales, even appearing as one of the Welsh emblems. For cooking, small, tender leeks are better than the huge ones. This soup can be roughly blended to give a hearty, country texture or blended until smooth and served with cream and snipped chives for a more luxurious soup. When served cold, potato and leek soup is known as 'Vichyssoise' – a really lovely soup to serve on a summer evening.

LEEK & POTATO SOUP

Serves 4–6

55 g/2 oz butter

1 onion, chopped

3 leeks, sliced

225 g/8 oz potatoes, peeled and cut into 2-cm/¾-inch cubes

850 ml/1½ pints vegetable stock

salt and pepper

to garnish

150 ml/5 fl oz single cream (optional)

2 tbsp snipped fresh chives

1 Melt the butter in a large saucepan over a medium heat, add the prepared vegetables and sauté gently for 2–3 minutes until soft but not brown. Pour in the stock, bring to the boil, then reduce the heat and simmer, covered, for 15 minutes.

2 Remove from the heat and liquidize the soup in the saucepan using a hand-held stick blender if you have one. Otherwise, pour into a blender, liquidize until smooth and return to the rinsed-out saucepan.

3 Heat the soup, season with salt and pepper to taste and serve in warm bowls, swirled with the cream, if using, and garnished with chives.

This Scottish soup is simply made with a whole chicken and leeks. Because the chicken is poached in the water, the resulting broth is highly flavoured. Some think the soup is better without the inclusion of prunes, which may date from medieval times, but their colour, texture and flavour give this soup its uniqueness. This is a main course, more like a stew, and as it is not blended it is quite rustic. By discarding the slow-cooked vegetables and adding fresh leeks, this soup takes on a fresh flavour and colour.

COCK-A-LEEKIE SOUP

Serves 6–8

- 2 tbsp vegetable or olive oil
- 2 onions, roughly chopped
- 2 carrots, roughly chopped
- 5 leeks, 2 roughly chopped, 3 sliced thinly
- 1 chicken, weighing 1.3 kg/3 lb
- 2 bay leaves
- salt and pepper
- 3 leeks, sliced finely
- 6 prunes, sliced
- 2 tbsp chopped fresh parsley, to garnish

1 Heat the oil in a large saucepan over a medium heat, and then add the onions, carrots and 2 roughly chopped leeks. Sauté for 3–4 minutes until just golden brown.

2 Wipe the chicken inside and out and remove any excess skin and fat.

3 Place the chicken in the saucepan with the cooked vegetables and add the bay leaves. Pour in enough cold water to just cover and season well with salt and pepper. Bring to the boil, reduce the heat, then cover and simmer for 1–1½ hours. Skim off any scum that forms from time to time.

4 Remove the chicken from the stock, skin, then remove all the meat. Cut the meat into neat pieces.

5 Drain the stock through a colander, discard the vegetables and bay leaves and return to the rinsed-out saucepan. Expect to have 1.2–1.4 litres/2–2½ pints of stock. If you have time, it is a good idea to allow the stock to cool so that the fat may be removed. If not, blot the fat off the surface with pieces of kitchen paper.

6 Heat the stock to simmering point, add the sliced leeks and prunes to the saucepan and heat for about 1 minute.

7 Return the chicken to the pan and heat through. Serve immediately in warm deep dishes garnished with the parsley.

Jerusalem artichokes are not related to the globe artichoke, and they do not come from Jerusalem. These knobbly root vegetables are a relation of the sunflower, and 'girasol', an old word for sunflower, was altered to 'Jerusalem'. For years they were not popular as they are difficult to peel, but there are newer varieties that are less knobbly and much easier to peel. The flavour is nutty and the texture produces a very creamy soup without the addition of cream. This soup is often called Palestine soup – for obvious reasons.

JERUSALEM ARTICHOKE SOUP

Serves 4–6

55 g/2 oz butter

2 onions, chopped

675 g/1½ lb Jerusalem artichokes, peeled and sliced

850 ml/1½ pints chicken or vegetable stock

300 ml/10 fl oz milk

salt and pepper

for the croûtons

2 slices day-old white bread, crusts removed

4 tbsp vegetable oil

1 To make the croûtons, cut the bread into 1-cm/½-inch cubes. Heat the oil in a frying pan and fry the croûtons in a single layer, tossing occasionally until they are golden brown and crisp. Remove the pan from the heat and spoon out the croûtons onto kitchen paper to drain. Use on the day of making.

2 Melt the butter in a large saucepan over a medium heat, add the onion and cook until soft.

3 Add the artichokes and mix well with the butter, cover the saucepan and sauté slowly over a low heat for about 10 minutes. Pour in the stock, bring to the boil, then reduce the heat and simmer, covered, for 20 minutes.

4 Remove from the heat and liquidize the soup in the saucepan using a hand-held stick blender if you have one. Otherwise, pour into a blender, liquidize until smooth and return to the rinsed-out saucepan. Stir in the milk and season with salt and pepper to taste.

5 Heat the soup until hot and serve with the crispy croûtons.

VARIATION

A luxury addition to this soup is to slice 4–6 fresh scallops and poach for 2–3 minutes in the finished soup until cooked through.

Mulligatawny soup is another Anglo-Indian dish flavoured with curry. The name 'Mulligatawny' comes from the Indian term for 'pepper water', which refers to the basic stock used. The wives of serving officers brought recipes from India back to Britain, where they became very popular long before the Indian take-away became the source of one of our favourite foods. The addition of apple is very good as the fruit complements the curry flavour, while the chopped coriander adds an authentic Indian taste.

MULLIGATAWNY SOUP

Serves 4–6

55 g/2 oz butter

2 onions, chopped

1 small turnip, cut into small dice

2 carrots, sliced finely

1 Cox's apple, cored, peeled and chopped

2 tbsp mild curry powder

1.2 litres/2 pints chicken stock

salt and pepper

juice of ½ lemon

175 g/6 oz cold cooked chicken, cut into small pieces

55 g/2 oz cooked rice

2 tbsp chopped fresh coriander

1 Melt the butter in a large saucepan over a medium heat, add the onion and sauté gently until soft but not brown.

2 Add the prepared vegetables and apple and continue to cook for a further few minutes.

3 Stir in the curry powder until the vegetables are well coated, then pour in the stock. Bring to the boil, cover and simmer for about 45 minutes. Season well with salt and pepper to taste and add the lemon juice.

4 Liquidize the soup with a hand-held stick blender in the saucepan. Alternatively, pour into a blender, liquidize until smooth and return to the rinsed-out saucepan. Add the chicken and coriander to the saucepan and heat through.

5 Serve in warm bowls with a spoonful of the rice in the base and the soup poured over the top. Garnish with the coriander.

VARIATION

I like this soup served cold in summer, when I add extra apple and a tablespoon of mango chutney.

Watercress is extremely rich in vitamins and iron. With its peppery flavour, watercress can often be used as an alternative to rocket: the leaves are fantastic stuffed into a grilled chicken and aïoli sandwich or a roast beef and horseradish roll. As well as making a great salad, it is wonderful cooked. In this recipe the watercress is used like baby spinach, the leaves added at the last minute to conserve all the flavour, goodness and colour. The addition of crème fraîche gives this classic vegetable soup a fresh modern taste.

WATERCRESS SOUP

Serves 4

2 bunches of watercress (approx 200 g/7 oz), thoroughly cleaned

40 g/1½ oz butter

2 onions, chopped

225 g/8 oz potatoes, peeled and roughly chopped

1.2 litres/2 pints vegetable stock or water

salt and pepper

whole nutmeg, for grating (optional)

125 ml/4 fl oz crème fraîche

1 Remove the leaves from the stalks of the watercress and keep on one side. Roughly chop the stalks.

2 Melt the butter in a large saucepan over a medium heat, add the onion and cook for 4–5 minutes until soft. Do not brown.

3 Add the potato to the saucepan and mix well with the onion. Add the watercress stalks and the stock.

4 Bring to the boil, then reduce the heat, cover and simmer for 15–20 minutes until the potato is soft.

5 Add the watercress leaves and stir in to heat through. Remove from the heat and use a hand-held stick blender to process the soup until smooth. Alternatively, liquidize the soup in a blender and return to the rinsed-out saucepan. Reheat and season with salt and pepper to taste, adding a good grating of nutmeg if using.

6 Serve in warm bowls with the crème fraîche spooned on top.

ANDREW'S

'Potting' is a method from pre-refrigerator days for preserving all sorts of meat and fish. More recently, it became a way of stretching extravagant ingredients a little further. The food is packed into small pots and covered with a layer of butter or other solid fat to exclude the air. As a Lancashire lass, I remember eating potted shrimps from Morecambe Bay, turning out the pots to see the pale brown shrimps embedded in lovely yellow butter, then eating them very slowly, savouring every morsel.

POTTED CRAB

Serves 4–6

1 large cooked crab, prepared by your fishmonger if possible

salt and pepper

whole nutmeg, for grating

2 pinches of cayenne pepper or mace

juice of 1 lemon

225 g/8 oz lightly salted butter

to serve

buttered toast slices

lemon wedges

1 If the crab is not already prepared, pick out all the meat, taking great care to remove all the meat from the claws.

2 Mix together the white and brown meat but do not mash too smoothly. Season well with salt and pepper and add a good grating of nutmeg and the cayenne pepper. Add the lemon juice to taste.

3 Melt half the butter in a saucepan and carefully mix in the crabmeat. Turn the mixture out into 4–6 small soufflé dishes or ramekins.

4 In a clean saucepan, heat the remaining butter until it melts, then continue heating for a few moments until it stops bubbling. Allow the sediment to settle and carefully pour the clarified butter over the crab mixture. This seal of clarified butter allows the potted crab to be kept for 1–2 days. Chill in the refrigerator for 1–2 hours.

5 Serve with lots of buttered toast and lemon wedges.

VARIATIONS

Shrimps, prawns, smoked salmon, smoked trout and smoked mackerel can also be potted in this way. As a great extravagance, lobster can be used.

Arbroath smokies are small Scottish haddock that have been hot-smoked to a rich brown colour and are usually sold in pairs. If you can't find Arbroath smokies, use cooked smoked haddock or smoked mackerel. The flavour of the smoked fish blends wonderfully with the cream and cheese. These make an unusual starter for a dinner party or a good supper. For a more substantial dish, I cook some pasta and place it in a large serving dish, top it with the fish and sauce mixture and heat for 20–25 minutes.

ARBROATH SMOKIE POTS

Serves 4

1 tbsp melted butter

350 g/12 oz Arbroath smokies or other smoked fish, skinned

2 hard-boiled eggs, chopped

pepper

25 g/1 oz butter

25 g/1 oz plain flour

300 ml/10 fl oz milk

55 g/2 oz Cheddar cheese, grated

salt

pinch of cayenne pepper

1 tbsp freshly grated Parmesan cheese

brown toast slices, to serve

1 Preheat the oven to 180°C/350°F/Gas Mark 4.

2 Use the melted butter to grease 4 small soufflé dishes or ramekins.

3 Flake the fish onto a plate, mix with the chopped egg and season with a little pepper. Place the mixture into the prepared dishes.

4 Melt the butter in a saucepan over a medium heat and stir in the flour. Cook for 1 minute, stirring continuously. Remove from the heat and stir in the milk gradually until smooth. Return to a low heat and stir until the sauce comes to the boil and thickens. Reduce the heat and simmer gently, stirring constantly, until the sauce is creamy and smooth.

5 Add the grated cheese and stir until melted, then season with salt and pepper to taste and add the cayenne pepper.

6 Pour the sauce over the fish and egg mixture and sprinkle over the grated Parmesan cheese.

7 Place the ramekins on a baking tray and cook in the oven for 10–15 minutes until bubbling and golden. Serve at once with brown toast.

Pâtés have been around for centuries and are a good way to stretch small quantities of meat or fish. Early versions were very often coarsely made by roughly chopping up the meat with seasonings and added fat. The advent of mechanical mincers and electric mixers resulted in smooth, silky-rich pâtés which are often served in small quantities as starters. I enjoy pâté as a main lunch or supper dish with lots of hot buttered toast or chunks of bread and some crisp celery or gherkins for added flavour and texture.

CHICKEN LIVER PATE

Serves 4

140 g/5 oz butter

1 onion, finely chopped

1 garlic clove, finely chopped

250 g/9 oz chicken livers

salt and pepper

½ tsp Dijon mustard

2 tbsp brandy (optional)

brown toast fingers, to serve

1 Melt half the butter in a large frying pan over a medium heat and cook the onion for 3–4 minutes until soft and transparent. Add the garlic and continue to cook for a further 2 minutes.

2 Check the chicken livers and remove any discoloured parts using a pair of scissors. Add the livers to the frying pan and cook over quite a high heat for 5–6 minutes until they are brown in colour.

3 Season well with salt and pepper and add the mustard and brandy, if using.

4 Process the pâté in a blender or food processor until smooth. Add the remaining butter cut into small pieces and process again until creamy.

5 Press the pâté into a serving dish or 4 small ramekins, smooth the surface and cover. If it is to be kept for more than 2 days, you could cover the surface with a little clarified butter (see page 55, step 4). Serve accompanied by toast fingers.

Of all the starters served in Britain, only the prawn cocktail has managed to achieve food icon status. It became popular as post-war austerity was replaced by restaurant dining, which for many meant a prawn cocktail followed by steak and chips. It has recently emerged from an unfashionable phase to find new popularity. The dressing can be created from home-made or bought mayonnaise and flavoured with spicy and tangy additions, but the key is to make the cocktail with the best ingredients available.

PRAWN COCKTAIL

Serves 4

½ iceberg lettuce, finely shredded

150 ml/5 fl oz mayonnaise

2 tbsp single cream

2 tbsp tomato ketchup

few drops of Tabasco sauce

juice of ½ lemon

salt and pepper

175 g/6 oz cooked peeled prawns

to garnish

dash of ground paprika

4 cooked prawns in their shells

4 lemon slices

thin buttered brown bread slices, to serve

1 Divide the lettuce between 4 small serving dishes (traditionally, stemmed glass ones, but any small dishes will be fine).

2 Mix together the mayonnaise, cream and tomato ketchup in a bowl. Add Tabasco and lemon juice to your taste and season well with salt and pepper.

3 Divide the peeled prawns equally between the dishes and pour over the dressing. Chill for 30 minutes in the refrigerator.

4 Sprinkle a little paprika over the cocktails and garnish with a prawn and a slice of lemon on each dish. Serve with the slices of brown bread and butter.

VARIATIONS

Other fish cocktails can be made in the same way. Try using crabmeat, lobster or a mixture of seafood. A more modern approach is to serve the prawns with avocado or mango and to add lime juice and fish sauce as flavourings, omitting the mayonnaise.

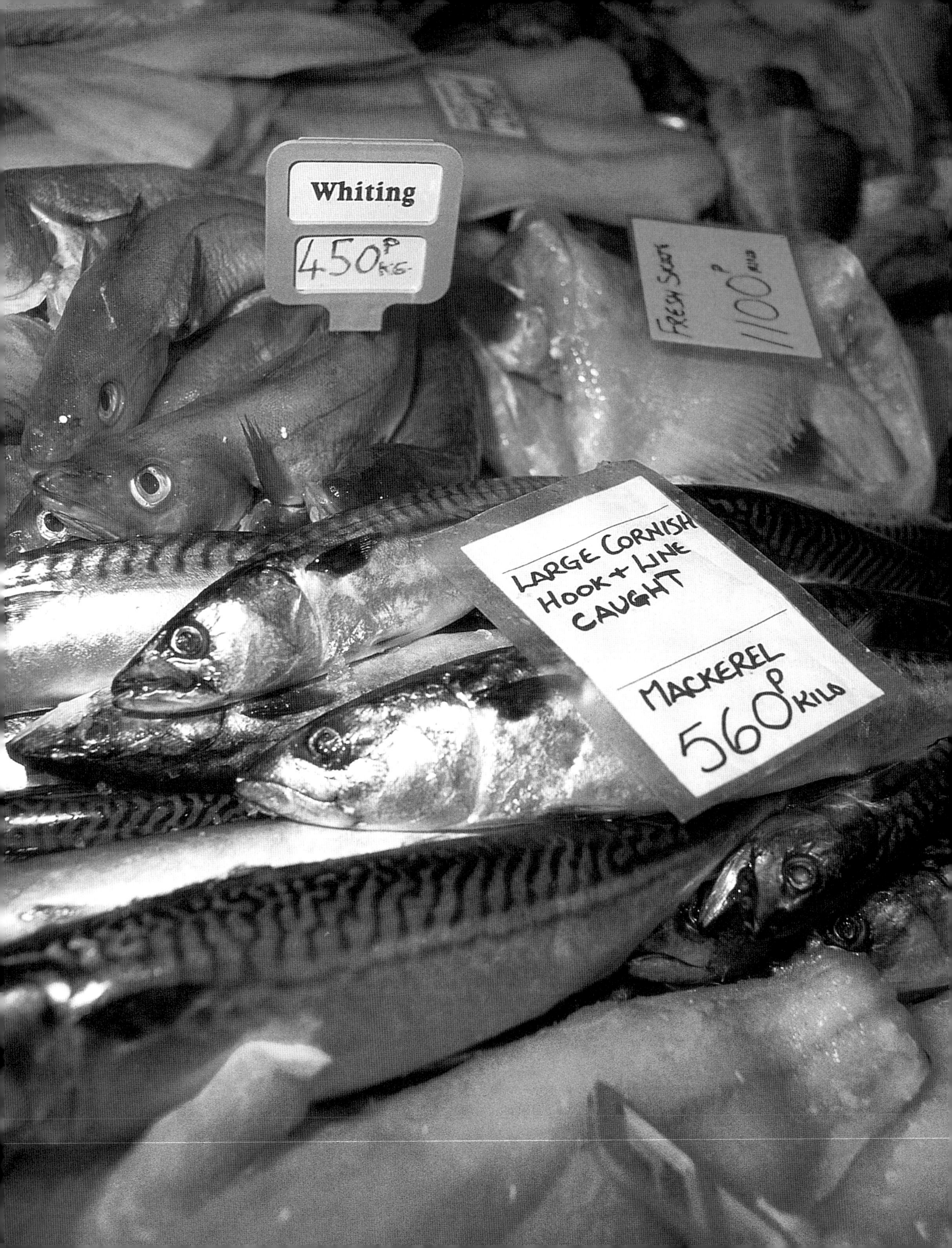

Whiting
450p KG
LARGE CORNISH
HOOK + LINE
CAUGHT
MACKEREL
560p KILO

3 FISH & SHELLFISH

As an island race, we have good access to all types of fish and shellfish. Sadly, we have not always valued them and quite a lot of our fish is now exported to France and further afield. For years our supplies of fresh fish have therefore been limited and often only available frozen. But suppliers are now realizing that we need to have fish as fresh as possible, preferably on the day they have been caught. A wide variety of fresh fish and shellfish is starting to become available, from sources as far apart as northern Scotland and Cornwall. Buying ready-prepared fish is often worthwhile when time is short, so you do not have to gut or fillet it yourself.

We seem to have retained our taste for fish despite the problems in getting hold of it, though perhaps this owes much to the timeless popularity of the fish-and-chip shop and one or two staples like fish fingers and fish cakes. I was brought up on these and they did me the world of good. Today our stocks of cod and haddock are getting low due to overfishing, but more exotic and unusual fish are now widely available, like tuna, swordfish and monkfish, and it is great to have our tastes broadened as we try different varieties. It is remarkable how popular fresh tuna has become. It was introduced to the British public after the Second World War, but they rejected it because they found it too much like meat. Now, however, now we can't seem to get enough of it. Possibly this is because we now travel more and our tastes are expanding, or perhaps we are just getting used to the fact that it is not like the canned variety. Certainly our tastes and cooking methods are changing – quickly griddled tuna is thought quite delicious, particularly when still pink in the centre.

Fish needs very little cooking so it is quick to prepare. It also provides us with a good supply of protein, contains little fat and is easily digested. Oily fish such as mackerel, herring, tuna, trout and salmon are rich in omega-3 fatty acids, which help to prevent heart disease and also reduce the amount of cholesterol in our blood. It is perhaps because of these health reasons that fish is rapidly growing in popularity. It is also versatile. Fish can be cooked by grilling, baking, steaming, frying and poaching. Served whole, stuffed, filleted, in steaks, battered, crumbed, in sauces or as a soup – the list is endless and the recipes innumerable. I'm sure we all have our favourites – mine are goujons of sole, and fish pie made with creamy mashed potato.

Some fish that were popular in the past have become less so. Jellied eels, cockles, winkles and whelks, which we used to buy at the seaside and enjoy as part of our holidays, are not the favourites they once were, whereas squid, sea bass, skate and scallops are now more popular than ever. Oysters, once food for the rich, are now more widely available and not too prohibitively expensive. Mussels are inexpensive and cook very quickly with hardly any preparation. Crabs and crab claws are more difficult to find but make a delicious summer lunch with mayonnaise and brown bread. The traditionally smoked fish, like cod and haddock, have been around for a long time and are still very popular.

Fish cakes used to be a popular children's tea-time meal, though ours were always frozen, a bit bland and in need of lots of ketchup. Now they have grown up and become trendy, the texture of fish chunks mixed with well-seasoned creamy potato and a crisp coating contrasting well to create a delicious and sophisticated meal. You can vary the fish used according to what is available. Smoked haddock is very tasty, while a mixture of smoked and fresh salmon provides a more sophisticated flavour.

FISH CAKES

Serves 4

450 g/1 lb floury potatoes, such as King Edwards, Maris Piper or Desirée, peeled and cut into chunks

450 g/1lb mixed fish fillets, such as cod and salmon, skinned

2 tbsp chopped fresh tarragon

grated rind of 1 lemon

2 tbsp double cream

salt and pepper

1 tbsp plain flour

1 egg, beaten

115 g/4 oz breadcrumbs, made from day-old white or wholemeal bread

4 tbsp vegetable oil, for frying

watercress salad, to serve

1 Cook the potatoes in a large saucepan of boiling salted water for 15–20 minutes. Drain well and mash with a potato masher until smooth.

2 Place the fish in a frying pan and just cover with water. Over a medium heat bring to the boil, then reduce the heat, cover and simmer gently for 5 minutes until cooked.

3 Remove from the heat and drain the fish onto a plate. When cool enough to handle, flake the fish roughly into good-sized pieces, ensuring that there are no bones.

4 Mix the potato with the fish, tarragon, lemon rind and cream. Season well with salt and pepper and shape into 4 round cakes or 8 smaller ones.

5 Dust the cakes with flour and dip them into the beaten egg. Coat thoroughly in the breadcrumbs. Place on a baking tray and allow to chill for at least 30 minutes.

6 Heat the oil in the frying pan and fry the cakes over medium heat for 5 minutes on each side, turning them carefully using a palette knife or a fish slice.

7 Serve with a crisp watercress salad, which complements the cakes well.

We tend to associate omelettes with France, but they have in fact been known since the sixteenth century in Britain. This omelette, named after the novelist Arnold Bennett, is rather an extravagant affair. The original version was devised in the 1930s by the chef of the Savoy Hotel in London for the author, who regularly dined there. It is said that Bennett liked it so much that he ordered it every time he visited the hotel. Some recipes add a hollandaise sauce to the haddock, cheese and cream, but I prefer it without.

OMELETTE ARNOLD BENNETT

Serves 2

175 g/6 oz undyed smoked haddock, skinned

25 g/1 oz butter

4 eggs

salt and pepper

1 tbsp olive oil

4 tbsp single cream

2 tbsp grated Cheddar or Parmesan cheese

1 Place the fish in a large saucepan and cover with water. Bring the water to the boil, then turn down to a simmer and poach the fish for 8–10 minutes until it flakes easily. Remove from the heat and drain onto a plate. When cool enough to handle, flake the fish and remove any bones.

2 Melt half the butter in a small saucepan and add the haddock, to warm.

3 Beat the eggs together gently with a fork and season carefully with the salt and pepper, taking care not to add too much salt because the haddock will already be quite salty.

4 Melt the remaining butter with the oil in a 23-cm/9-inch frying pan over a medium heat. When the butter starts to froth, pour in the eggs and spread them around by tilting the frying pan. Use a spatula or fork to move the egg around until it is cooked underneath but still liquid on top.

5 Tip in the hot haddock and spread over the omelette.

6 Pour over the cream and top with the cheese, then place the frying pan under a hot grill for 1 minute until the cheese is melted. Serve immediately on hot plates.

VARIATIONS

You can make individual omelettes using a smaller pan and 2–3 eggs per person. A more elaborate omelette can also be made with the addition of hollandaise sauce (see page 77).

Fish pie has been popular comfort food for a long time, but it is a very fine dish when made with good ingredients and one or two added extras. The basic fish is usually a white fish such as plaice, while the addition of some prawns adds to the luxury feel of the pie, as do the mushrooms and fresh herbs. A creamy sauce made with the fish stock and some wine, enriched with cream, makes this a truly special dish. Topped with creamy mashed potato, you have a pie worthy of any dinner party table.

FISHERMAN'S PIE

Serves 6

butter, for greasing

900 g/2 lb white fish fillets, such as plaice, skinned

salt and pepper

150 ml/¼ pint dry white wine

1 tbsp chopped fresh parsley, tarragon or dill

175 g/6 oz small mushrooms, sliced

110 g/3½ oz butter

175 g/6 oz cooked peeled prawns

40 g/1½ oz plain flour

125 ml/4 fl oz double cream

900 g/2 lb floury potatoes, such as King Edwards, Maris Piper or Desirée, peeled and cut into chunks

1 Preheat the oven to 180°C/350°F/Gas Mark 4. Butter a 1.7-litre/3-pint baking dish.

2 Fold the fish fillets in half and place in the dish. Season well with salt and pepper, pour over the wine and scatter over the herbs.

3 Cover with foil and bake for 15 minutes until the fish starts to flake. Strain off the liquid and reserve for the sauce. Increase the oven temperature to 220°C/425°F/Gas Mark 7.

4 Sauté the mushrooms in a frying pan with 15 g/½ oz of the butter and spoon over the fish. Scatter over the prawns.

5 Heat 55 g/2 oz of the butter in a saucepan and stir in the flour. Cook for a few minutes without browning, remove from the heat, then add the reserved cooking liquid gradually, stirring well between each addition.

6 Return to the heat and gently bring to the boil, still stirring to ensure a smooth sauce. Add the cream and season to taste with salt and pepper. Pour over the fish in the dish and smooth over the surface.

7 Make the mashed potato by cooking the potatoes in boiling salted water for 15–20 minutes. Drain well and mash with a potato masher until smooth. Season to taste with salt and pepper and add the remaining butter, stirring until melted.

8 Pile or pipe the potato onto the fish and sauce and bake for 10–15 minutes until golden brown.

Creamy fish and flaky pastry is a marriage made in heaven. This recipe suggests using white fish fillets, but you can use other fish if you prefer – a mixture of haddock and smoked haddock is good. The addition of prawns or mussels also works well. England's most famous fish pie came from Cornwall and was called 'Stargazey Pie'. It consisted of small pilchards or herrings, still with their heads on, baked in a pie with the fish heads sticking up through the pastry 'gazing star-wards'!

FLAKY PASTRY FISH PIE

Serves 4–6

butter, for greasing

650 g/1 lb 7 oz white fish fillets, such as cod or haddock, skinned

300 ml/½ pint milk

1 bay leaf

4 peppercorns

1 small onion, finely sliced

40 g/1½ oz butter

40 g/1½ oz plain flour, plus extra for dusting

salt and pepper

1 tbsp chopped fresh parsley or tarragon

150 ml/5 fl oz single cream

2 hard-boiled eggs, roughly chopped

400 g/14 oz ready-made puff pastry

1 egg, beaten

1 Preheat the oven to 200°C/400°F/Gas Mark 6. Butter a 1.2-litre/2-pint pie dish.

2 Place the fish in a frying pan and cover with the milk. Add the bay leaf, peppercorns and onion slices. Bring to the boil, reduce the heat and simmer gently for 10–12 minutes.

3 Remove from the heat and strain off the milk into a measuring jug. Add a little extra milk if necessary to make the liquid up to 300 ml/½ pint. Take out the fish and flake into large pieces, removing any bones.

4 Melt the butter in a saucepan and add the flour. Stir well and cook over a low heat for 2–3 minutes. Remove from the heat and gradually stir in the reserved milk, beating well after each addition. Return the pan to the heat and cook, stirring continuously, until thickened. Continue to cook for 2–3 minutes until smooth and glossy. Season to taste, add the herbs and cream.

5 Place the fish in the bottom of the pie dish, then add the egg and season with salt and pepper. Pour the sauce over the fish and mix carefully.

6 Roll out the pastry on a lightly floured surface until just larger than the pie dish. Cut off a strip 1 cm/½ inch wide from around the edge. Moisten the rim of the dish with water and press the pastry strip onto it. Moisten the pastry collar and put on the pastry lid. Crimp the edges firmly and glaze with the egg. If desired, garnish with the leftover pastry shaped into leaves.

7 Place the pie on a baking tray and bake near the top of the oven for 20–25 minutes. Cover with foil if getting too brown.

Grilling or barbecuing fish is one of the best ways to preserve all its flavour, particularly when it has been freshly landed at a British fishing port. Whole freshwater fish, preferably caught yourself, is also very good cooked simply on a grill or even on the spot over an open wood fire – the added aroma of the woodsmoke and the crispy skin are delicious bonuses. To enhance the taste, the fish should be gutted and cleaned and a mixture of subtle herbs and flavourings stuffed into the body cavity.

GRILLED MUSHROOM & SPINACH-STUFFED TROUT

Serves 2

2 whole trout, about 350 g/12 oz each, gutted

1 tbsp vegetable oil

salt and pepper

for the stuffing

25 g/1 oz butter

2 shallots, finely chopped

55 g/2 oz mushrooms, finely chopped

55 g/2 oz baby spinach

1 tbsp chopped fresh parsley or tarragon

grated rind of 1 lemon

whole nutmeg, for grating

for the tomato salsa

2 tomatoes, peeled, deseeded and finely diced

10-cm/4-inch piece of cucumber, finely diced

2 spring onions, finely chopped

1 tbsp olive oil

salt and pepper

1 Clean the trout, trim the fins with a pair of scissors and wipe the inside of the fish with kitchen paper. Leave the head and tail on and slash the skin of each fish on both sides about 5 times. Brush with the oil and season well with salt and pepper, both inside and out.

2 To make the stuffing, melt the butter in a small saucepan and gently soften the shallots for 2–3 minutes. Add the mushrooms and continue to cook for a further 2 minutes. Add the spinach and heat until it is just wilted.

3 Remove from the heat and add the herbs, lemon rind and a good grating of nutmeg. Allow to cool.

4 Fill the trout with the mushroom and spinach stuffing, then reshape them as neatly as you can.

5 Grill under a medium grill for 10–12 minutes, turning once. The skin should be brown and crispy. Alternatively, barbecue for 6–8 minutes on each side, depending on the heat.

6 To make the tomato salsa, mix together all the ingredients and season well with the salt and pepper.

7 Serve the trout hot with the tomato salsa spooned over them.

Salmon has always been known as the king of fish and is very versatile. A whole salmon makes a stunning centrepiece for a buffet or a family celebration and is one of those classic summer party dishes that makes a perfect partner for sparkling wine. This recipe poaches the whole salmon in the oven rather than in a fish kettle on the hob, and is suitable for fish under 2.25 kg/5 lb in weight. However, if you do own a fish kettle, the traditional method works just as well.

POACHED SALMON WITH QUICK HOLLANDAISE SAUCE

Serves 8

melted butter, for greasing

1.8 kg/4 lb whole fresh salmon, gutted

salt and pepper

1 lemon, sliced

few sprigs of fresh parsley

125 ml/4 fl oz white wine or water

for the quick hollandaise sauce

2 tbsp white wine vinegar

2 tbsp water

6 black peppercorns

3 egg yolks

250 g/9 oz unsalted butter

2 tsp lemon juice

salt and pepper

1 Preheat the oven to 150°C/300°F/Gas Mark 2. Line a large roasting tin with a double layer of foil and brush with butter.

2 Trim off the fins then season the salmon with salt and pepper, inside and out. Lay on the foil and place the lemon slices and parsley in the body cavity. Pour over the wine and gather up the foil to make a fairly loose parcel.

3 Bake for 50–60 minutes. Test the salmon with the point of a knife: the flesh should flake when the fish is cooked. Remove from the oven and leave to stand for 15 minutes before removing from the foil to serve hot. To serve cold, leave for 1–2 hours until lukewarm then carefully remove from the foil and peel away the skin from the top side, leaving the head and tail intact.

4 Meanwhile, to make the hollandaise sauce, put the wine vinegar and water into a small saucepan with the peppercorns, bring to the boil, then reduce the heat and simmer until it is reduced to 1 tablespoon (take care, this happens very quickly). Strain.

5 Mix the egg yolks in a blender or food processor and add the strained vinegar while the machine is running.

6 Melt the butter in a small saucepan and heat until it almost turns brown. Again, while the blender is running, add three-quarters of the butter, the lemon juice, then the remaining butter and season well with salt and pepper.

7 Turn the sauce into a serving bowl or keep warm for up to 1 hour in a bowl over a pan of warm water. To serve cold, allow to cool and store in the refrigerator for up to 2 days. Serve the sauce on the side with the salmon.

Roasting is my favourite way to serve a whole fish – it not only looks good, it picks up other flavours beautifully. You can use either small individual fish to serve as single portions or one large one to share among family or friends. Round fish like sea bass, sea bream, red mullet, red snapper, trout and mackerel are particularly good for roasting as their skin crisps up well while the flesh stays deliciously moist and creamy. Make sure you use really fresh fish if you want this dish to sparkle.

ROASTED SEA BASS

Serves 4

1.3–1.8 kg/3–4 lb whole sea bass, gutted

salt and pepper

1 small onion, finely chopped

2 garlic cloves, finely chopped

2 tbsp finely chopped fresh herbs, such as parsley, chervil and tarragon

25 g/1 oz anchovy fillets, finely chopped

25 g/1 oz butter

150 ml/¼ pint white wine

2 tbsp crème fraîche

1 Preheat the oven to 200°C/400°F/Gas Mark 6.

2 Remove any scales from the fish and clean it thoroughly both inside and out. If desired, trim off the fins with a pair of scissors. Using a sharp knife, make five or six cuts diagonally into the flesh of the fish on both sides. Season well with salt and pepper, both inside and out.

3 Mix the onion, garlic, herbs and anchovies together in a bowl.

4 Stuff the fish with half the mixture and spoon the remainder into a roasting tin. Place the bass on top.

5 Spread the butter over the bass, pour over the wine and place in the oven. Roast for 30–35 minutes until the fish is cooked through.

6 Remove the fish from the tin to a warmed serving dish. Return the tin to the top of the stove and stir the onion mixture and juices together over a medium heat. Add the crème fraîche and pour into a warmed serving bowl.

7 Serve the sea bass whole and divide at the table. Spoon a little sauce on the side.

VARIATION

Red mullet, weighing 280–350 g/10–12 oz each, will take only 15–20 minutes to roast. Serve 1 per person. Brush well with butter and stuff simply with some herbs and lemon slices.

Scallops are the most delicate of shellfish, creamy in texture and with a sweet flavour. They hardly need any cooking so are ideal for a quick supper, and although expensive you don't need many: 3–4 per person are sufficient. In the past, scallops tended to be served with rich sauces, but today simplicity is the key and a quick sear in a hot frying pan or on a griddle is all they need. Most scallops come with their orange coral. You can cook these at the same time or keep them (frozen) to flavour fish pies or sauces.

SCALLOPS WITH HERB BUTTER

Serves 3–4

12 large shelled scallops, cleaned

salt and pepper

1 tbsp vegetable oil

crusty bread, to serve

for the herb butter

25 g/1 oz unsalted butter

2 garlic cloves, finely chopped

2 tbsp chopped fresh parsley

1 Cut away any discoloured parts from the scallops. Dry well and season with salt and pepper.

2 Heat a heavy-based frying pan or griddle and brush with the oil. When the oil is smoking, add the scallops and cook for 1 minute, then turn and cook on the other side for 1 minute. It is a good idea to cook the scallops in 2 batches, as if you try to cook them all at once you might end up with them stewing rather than frying. The scallops should have a good golden colour and a slight crust at the edges. Transfer to a warm plate and keep warm.

3 To make the herb butter, melt the butter in a saucepan and fry the garlic for a few seconds. Add the parsley and, while still foaming, pour over the scallops.

4 Serve at once with plenty of crusty bread to mop up the juices.

VARIATION

Scallops with Crushed Beans and Rocket Salad

Fry 1 finely chopped garlic clove in 1 tablespoon olive oil in a small saucepan. Add a pinch of dried crushed chillies and mix well. Drain 400 g/14 oz canned flageolet beans and add to the pan with 125 ml/4 fl oz white wine. Bring to the boil and crush the beans with a wooden spoon until you have a rough paste, adding a little water to make a loose purée, and season with salt and pepper to taste. Divide the purée among 4 warm serving dishes and place the cooked scallops on top. Serve with a rocket salad dressed simply with olive oil and lemon juice.

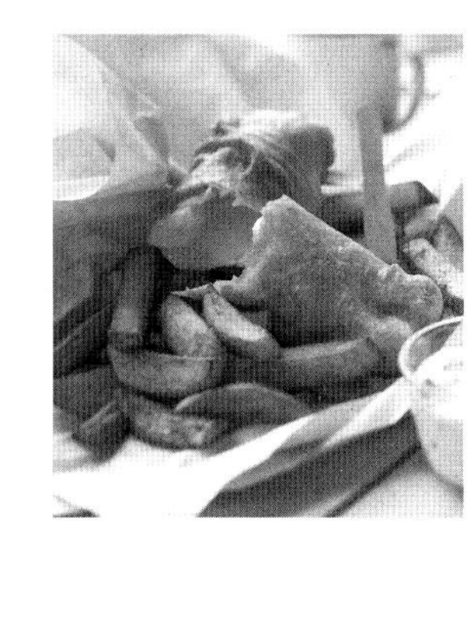

Our great national dish, fish and chips, always seems to feature in childhood memories of food – the time you stayed up to go with an older brother or sister to buy a late supper, or that wet holiday when, drenched to the skin, you bought a warm handful of fish and chips to eat while the rain streamed down your neck. I have a friend who always has the ultimate birthday supper: fish and chips on the beach with a bottle of champagne. Try making fish and chips yourself – you will find the home-cooked version totally delicious.

FISH & CHIPS

Serves 2

vegetable oil, for deep-frying

3 large potatoes, such as Cara or Desirée

2 thick cod or haddock fillets, 175 g/6 oz each

salt and pepper

175 g/6 oz self-raising flour, plus extra for dusting

200 ml/7 fl oz cold lager

tartare sauce, to serve

1 Heat the oil in a temperature-controlled deep-fat fryer to 120°C/250°F, or in a heavy-based saucepan, checking the temperature with a thermometer, to blanch the chips. Preheat the oven to 150°C/300°F/Gas Mark 2.

2 Peel the potatoes and cut into even-sized chips. Fry for about 8–10 minutes, depending on size, until softened but not coloured. Remove from the oil, drain on kitchen paper and place in a warm dish in the warm oven. Increase the temperature of the oil to 180–190°C/350–375°F, or until a cube of bread browns in 30 seconds.

3 Meanwhile, season the fish with salt and pepper and dust it lightly with a little flour.

4 Make a thick batter by sieving the flour into a bowl with a little salt and whisking in most of the lager. Check the consistency before adding the remainder: it should be very thick like double cream.

5 Dip one fillet into the batter and allow the batter to coat it thickly. Carefully place the fish in the hot oil, then repeat with the other fillet.

6 Cook for 8–10 minutes, depending on the thickness of the fish. Turn the fillets over halfway through the cooking time. Remove the fish from the fryer or saucepan, drain and keep warm.

7 Make sure the oil temperature is still at 180°C/350°F and return the chips to the fryer or saucepan. Cook for a further 2–3 minutes until golden brown and crispy. Drain and season with salt and pepper before serving with the battered fish and tartare sauce.

PALACE
PALACE

Dublin Bay prawns are also known as langoustines or scampi. Breaded and fried scampi are a great favourite with the British, but fresh Dublin Bay prawns are now also more readily available from Scotland and abroad. You can, however, use large Mediterranean or tiger prawns if you can't find langoustines. Dublin Bay prawns are simply delicious served grilled or fried in herb butter, with a little salad and a glass of cold Sauvignon. In seaside pubs they are sometimes served cold in a pint glass and washed down with beer.

GARLIC & HERB DUBLIN BAY PRAWNS

Serves 2

12 raw Dublin Bay prawns in their shells

juice of ½ lemon

2 garlic cloves, crushed

3 tbsp chopped fresh parsley

1 tbsp chopped fresh dill

3 tbsp softened butter

salt and pepper

to serve

lemon wedges

crusty bread

salad

1 Rinse and peel the prawns. Devein, using a sharp knife to slice along the back from the head end to the tail, and removing the thin black intestine.

2 Mix the lemon juice with the garlic, herbs and butter to form a paste. Season well with the salt and pepper. Spread the paste over the prawns and leave to marinate for 30 minutes.

3 Cook the prawns under a preheated medium grill for 5–6 minutes. Alternatively, heat a frying pan and fry the prawns in the paste until cooked. Turn out onto hot plates and pour over the pan juices. Serve at once with lemon wedges, some crusty bread and a salad.

Cook's tip

Some people prefer to leave the shells on the prawns so that they can suck the crunchy shells before peeling them off and eating the flesh with their fingers. Perhaps this is best kept for a cosy supper *à deux*!

VARIATIONS

To make a more substantial meal, serve the prawns with some fine spaghetti or angel hair pasta. Dublin Bay prawns can also be served cold in a salad. Try mixing 125 g/4½ oz cooked Dublin Bay prawns with 280 g/10 oz cubed melon and a cubed avocado. Dress with 4 tablespoons lime juice and 1 tablespoon Thai fish sauce and add a pinch of sugar. Mix well and garnish with chopped fresh coriander.

Lightly fried, tiny silvery whitebait were once considered a great delicacy, so fashionable that grand dinners were held at Greenwich to celebrate them. Now they are generally available frozen and are a lot more widely accessible. Interestingly, they are only eaten in Britain as they are not known anywhere else. Whitebait are the young of herrings and sprats and are eaten whole. 'Devilled' refers to the addition of cayenne pepper in this recipe. If you don't want your whitebait spicy, just leave it out.

DEVILLED WHITEBAIT

Serves 4

675 g/1½ lb whitebait, defrosted if frozen

4 tbsp milk

55 g/2 oz plain flour

salt and pepper

vegetable oil, for deep-frying

to serve

cayenne pepper (optional)

lemon wedges

buttered brown bread slices

1 Make sure the fish are clean and remove any very small bits of fish.

2 Place the fish in a bowl, pour in the milk and turn the fish over so that they have a coating of milk.

3 Drain, place the whitebait in a large plastic bag with the flour and season with salt and pepper. Shake the bag gently until the fish are well coated.

4 Heat the oil in a heavy-based saucepan or deep-fat fryer to a temperature of 180–190°C/350–375°F, or until a cube of bread browns in 30 seconds.

5 Place the whitebait in the hot oil and fry in 2–3 batches for 2 minutes until crisp and golden brown. They should be separate and not stick together. Drain on kitchen paper and keep hot while frying the remaining batches.

6 Serve hot with a dusting of cayenne pepper, if using, wedges of lemon and the buttered bread slices.

4

MEAT, GAME & POULTRY

Meat is the traditional mainstay of a British meal. We all remember family Sunday lunches, with roast beef and Yorkshire pudding or roast leg of pork with apple sauce. I recall the wonderful smells coming from the kitchen beforehand, but also the washing up that had to be done afterwards. The week's menus used to be arranged around the joint. Roast on Sunday, cold on Monday, shepherd's pie on Tuesday, curry on Wednesday and rissoles on Thursday (fish on Friday). Roasting is still a popular method of cooking meat because it makes it tender and enhances the flavours. Beef, pork and lamb are the most important meats in Britain, but roast chicken is now universally the most popular roast. Poultry has become more popular as people are eating less red meat. Game includes pheasant, grouse, rabbit and venison and has grown in popularity with its wider availability.

Casual midweek meals tend to use smaller cuts of meat, such as chops, steaks and chicken joints, which are quick to cook and need little preparation. Minced meat is also popular, particularly in cottage and shepherd's pie and in that dish which is very popular, but hardly a traditional British recipe – spaghetti bolognese.

In the past we have eaten all parts of an animal, including head, tail, feet, liver, kidneys, brain, ears, tongue, heart, lungs, and other bits I won't mention. Known as offal, these are now quite popular again, with even pigs' trotters back on the menu at many fashionable restaurants.

Poultry is the word used to describe those birds that are reared for the table: chickens, ducks and turkeys. They are available whole and in joints – legs, thighs, drumsticks and breasts, which can all be used in recipes for one to two people or for larger groups. Roasting or grilling is particularly suitable for these products. The poultry industry has increased in size dramatically over the last few years as people have responded to the medical world's exhortation to eat more healthily, increasing the demand for white meat as opposed to red meat.

Producers have also been rearing better quality birds with fuller flavours – organic and free-range birds having the best taste of all. They are also providing us with a wider choice: Barbary ducks for example, which have a plumper breast than the traditional Aylesbury duck.

Game, in its various forms, is also more widely available. Rabbit and venison are lean, healthy meats with lots of flavour. Pheasants are in season from October to February and grouse from August ('the glorious twelfth') until December. Whole pheasants and grouse can be roasted, but can also be jointed and used in casseroles to ensure they are tender. The season for deer-hunting is from late June until January, but most game is now farmed and available all year round.

We are fortunate in our supply of meat, poultry and game, despite food scares like BSE, and foot-and-mouth disease. More producers are giving us free-range or organic meat, and traditional breeds of cattle and pigs are being reintroduced, such as Aberdeen Angus and Herefordshire cattle, and Gloucester Old Spot, Saddleback and Middle White pigs.

Roast beef is probably the meal for which the British are known best around the world. Old paintings show the feasts of Tudor times, featuring huge ribs of beef served at Court; magnificent, and just how beef ought to be served. Roast beef is the most difficult roast to get right, because, unlike other meats, you need to cook it so that it is still pink in the centre: careful timing is all. The best roast beef is a rib cooked on the bone, but this must be a good size.

ROAST BEEF

Serves 8

2.7 kg/6 lb prime rib of beef

salt and pepper

2 tsp dry English mustard

3 tbsp plain flour

300 ml/½ pint red wine

300 ml/½ pint beef stock

2 tsp Worcestershire sauce (optional)

Yorkshire Pudding (see Accompaniment), to serve

ACCOMPANIMENT

Yorkshire Pudding

Preheat the oven to 220°C/425°F/Gas Mark 7. Make a batter with 100 g/3½ oz plain flour, a pinch of salt, 1 beaten egg and 300 ml/10 fl oz milk and water mixed. Allow to stand for half an hour. Heat 2 tbsp roast beef dripping or olive oil in a 20-cm/8-inch square roasting tin in the top of the oven. Remove the tin from the oven, pour in the batter and bake for 25-30 minutes until it is puffed up and golden brown. Serves 4.

1 Preheat the oven to 230°C/450°F/Gas Mark 8.

2 Season the meat with the salt and pepper and rub in the mustard and 1 tablespoon of the flour.

3 Place the meat in a roasting tin large enough to hold it comfortably and roast for 15 minutes. Reduce the heat to 190°C/375°F/Gas Mark 5 and cook for 15 minutes per 450 g/1 lb, plus 15 minutes (1 hour 45 minutes for this joint) for rare beef or 20 minutes per 450 g/1 lb, plus 20 minutes (2 hours 20 minutes) for medium beef. Baste the meat from time to time to keep it moist and if the tin becomes too dry, add a little stock or red wine.

4 Remove the meat from the oven and place on a hot serving plate, cover with foil and leave in a warm place for 10–15 minutes.

5 To make the gravy, pour off most of the fat from the tin (reserve it for the Yorkshire pudding), leaving behind the meat juices and the sediment. Place the tin on the top of the stove over a medium heat and scrape all the sediments from the base of the tin. Sprinkle in the remaining flour and quickly mix it into the juices with a small whisk. When you have a smooth paste, gradually add the wine and most of the stock, whisking all the time. Bring to the boil, then turn down the heat to a gentle simmer and cook for 2–3 minutes. Season with salt and pepper and add the remaining stock, if needed, and a little Worcestershire sauce, if liked.

6 When ready to serve, carve the meat into slices and serve on hot plates. Pour the gravy into a warm jug and take direct to the table. Serve with Yorkshire pudding.

Roast pork can be delicious or disappointing. It is all to do with the quality of the pork and whether the fat will 'crackle' properly. The crackling is all important. It is the favourite part of the joint and unless it is crisp and crunchy the whole meal will be a disappointment. The best joints of pork for roasting are the leg and the loin. Choose the leg if you are catering for large numbers, although the loin, which can be bought in smaller sizes, is the best for crackling.

ROAST PORK WITH CRACKLING

Serves 4

1 kg/2 lb 4 oz piece of pork loin, boned and the skin removed and reserved

salt and pepper

2 tbsp mustard

Apple Sauce (see Accompaniment), to serve

for the gravy

1 tbsp flour

300 ml/10 fl oz cider, apple juice or stock

ACCOMPANIMENT

Apple Sauce

Peel, core and slice 450 g/1 lb Bramley apples into a medium saucepan. Add 3 tablespoons water and 15 g/½ oz caster sugar and cook over a gentle heat for 10 minutes, stirring from time to time. A little ground cinnamon could be added, as could 15 g/½ oz butter, if desired. Beat well until the sauce is thick and smooth – use a hand mixer for a really smooth finish.

1 Preheat the oven to 200°C/400°F/Gas Mark 6.

2 Make sure the skin of the pork is well scored and sprinkle with the salt. Place on a wire rack on a baking tray and roast for 30–40 minutes until the crackling is golden brown and crispy. This can be cooked in advance, leaving room in the oven for roast potatoes.

3 Season the loin of pork well with salt and pepper and spread the fat with the mustard. Place in a roasting tin and roast in the centre of the oven for 20 minutes. Reduce the oven temperature to 190°C/375°F/Gas Mark 5 and cook for 50–60 minutes until the meat is a good colour and the juices run clear when pierced with a skewer.

4 Remove the meat from the oven and place on a hot serving plate, cover with foil and leave in a warm place.

5 To make the gravy, pour off most of the fat from the roasting tin, leaving the meat juices and the sediments. Sprinkle in the flour, whisking well. Cook the paste for a couple of minutes, then add the cider a little at a time until you have a smooth gravy. Boil for 2–3 minutes until it is the required consistency. Season well with salt and pepper and pour into a hot serving jug.

6 Carve the pork into slices and serve on hot plates with pieces of the crackling and the gravy. Accompany with apple sauce.

If you want a roast for two, a rack of lamb is ideal. It is quick and simple to cook and provides delicious meat, full of flavour. Lamb is best in spring, from Easter onwards, when it is at its sweetest and most succulent. Rosemary and garlic are traditional flavourings and a gravy made with red wine and redcurrant jelly is divine. Fresh mint for sauce is also at its best around this time. Rack of lamb is an impressive dish for entertaining too. Just double or treble the ingredients, depending on the number of guests.

RACK OF LAMB

Serves 2

1 trimmed rack of lamb (approximately 250–300 g/9–10 oz rack)

1 garlic clove, crushed

150 ml/¼ pint red wine

1 sprig of fresh rosemary, crushed to release the flavour

salt and pepper

1 tbsp olive oil

150 ml/¼ pint lamb stock

2 tbsp redcurrant jelly

Mint Sauce (see Accompaniment), to serve

1 Place the rack of lamb in a non-metallic bowl and rub all over with the garlic. Pour over the wine and place the rosemary sprig on top. Cover and leave to marinate in the fridge for 3 hours or overnight if possible.

2 Preheat the oven to 220°C/425°F/Gas Mark 7.

3 Remove the lamb from the marinade, reserving the marinade, dry the meat with kitchen paper and season well with salt and pepper. Put in a small roasting tin, drizzle with the oil and roast for 15–20 minutes, depending on whether you like your meat pink or medium. Remove the lamb from the oven and leave to rest, covered with foil, in a warm place for 5 minutes.

4 Put the marinade into a small pan, bring to the boil over a medium heat and bubble away for 2–3 minutes. Add the lamb stock and redcurrant jelly and simmer until a syrupy consistency is achieved.

5 Carve the lamb into cutlets and serve on warmed plates with the sauce spooned over the top. Serve the mint sauce separately.

ACCOMPANIMENT

Mint Sauce

Chop a small bunch of fresh mint leaves with 2 teaspoons caster sugar and place in a small bowl. Add 2 tablespoons boiling water and stir to dissolve the sugar. Add 2 tablespoons white wine vinegar and leave to stand for 30 minutes before serving with the lamb.

Chicken has become a well-established favourite in recent years, though it was once seen as quite exclusive. Simply roasted, with lots of thyme and lemon, chicken produces a succulent gastronomic feast for many occasions. Try to buy a good fresh chicken as frozen birds do not have as much flavour. You can stuff your chicken with a traditional stuffing, such as sage and onion, or fruit like apricots and prunes, but often the best way is to keep it simple.

ROAST CHICKEN

Serves 6

2.25 kg/5 lb free-range chicken

55 g/2 oz butter

2 tbsp chopped fresh lemon thyme

salt and pepper

1 lemon, quartered

125 ml/4 fl oz white wine

6 sprigs of fresh thyme, to garnish

1 Preheat the oven to 220°C/425°F/Gas Mark 7.

2 Make sure the chicken is clean, wiping it inside and out using kitchen paper, and place in a roasting tin.

3 In a bowl, soften the butter with a fork, mix in the herbs and season well with salt and pepper.

4 Butter the chicken all over with the herb butter, inside and out, and place the lemon pieces inside the body cavity. Pour the wine over the chicken.

5 Roast in the centre of the oven for 20 minutes. Reduce the temperature to 190°C/375°F/Gas Mark 5 and continue to roast for a further 1¼ hours, basting frequently. Cover with foil if the skin begins to brown too much. If the tin dries out, add a little more wine or water.

6 Test that the chicken is cooked by piercing the thickest part of the leg with a sharp knife or skewer and making sure the juices run clear. Remove from the oven.

7 Remove the chicken from the roasting tin and place on a warm serving plate, covered with foil, to rest for 10 minutes before carving.

8 Place the roasting tin on the top of the stove and bubble the pan juices gently over a low heat until they have reduced and are thick and glossy. Season with salt and pepper to taste.

9 Serve the chicken with the pan juices and scatter with the thyme sprigs.

Roast gammon or ham has long been a favourite choice for Sunday lunch and for Boxing Day dinner. Both gammon and ham are salted, either by salt curing or soaking in brine, and some varieties, like York ham, can be smoked. Some joints may need to be soaked in water for 2 hours or overnight to reduce the saltiness (check with your butcher, or on the packaging, to see if it has been pre-soaked). The sweet glaze of hams, or the serving of a sweet accompaniment like Cumberland sauce, is to counteract the salt.

ROAST GAMMON

Serves 6

1.3 kg/3 lb boneless gammon, pre-soaked if necessary

2 tbsp Dijon mustard

85 g/3 oz demerara sugar

½ tsp ground cinnamon

½ tsp ground ginger

18 whole cloves

Cumberland Sauce (see Accompaniment), to serve

1 Place the joint in a large saucepan, cover with cold water and slowly bring to the boil over a gentle heat. Cover and simmer very gently for 1 hour.

2 Preheat the oven to 200°C/400°F/Gas Mark 6.

3 Remove the gammon from the pan and drain. Remove the rind from the gammon and discard. Score the fat into a diamond-shaped pattern with a sharp knife.

4 Spread the mustard over the fat. Mix together the sugar and the spices on a plate and roll the gammon in it, pressing down well to coat evenly.

5 Stud the diamond shapes with cloves and place the joint in a roasting tin. Roast for 20 minutes until the glaze is a rich golden colour.

6 To serve hot, allow to stand for 20 minutes before carving. If the gammon is to be served cold, it can be cooked a day ahead. Serve with Cumberland sauce.

ACCOMPANIMENT

Cumberland Sauce

Using a lemon zester, remove the zest of 2 oranges (Seville, when in season, are the best). Place 4 tablespoons redcurrant jelly in a small saucepan with 4 tablespoons port and 1 teaspoon mustard and heat gently until the jelly is melted. Cut the oranges in half and squeeze the juice into the pan. Add the orange zest and season with salt and pepper to taste. Serve cold with gammon. The sauce can be kept in a screw-top jar in the refrigerator for up to 2 weeks.

Duck is wonderful to serve on a special occasion, the only drawback being that there is not much meat on the bird and it can be difficult to carve. Why not have your butcher bone the duck for you and then stuff it with good-quality sausage meat? I also add a couple of duck breasts to make a very substantial dish for 6–8 people that is easy to carve and looks wonderful. Serve with a sweet sauce: orange is classic, but I prefer to make one with canned apricots, spiced with cinnamon and ginger.

BONED & STUFFED ROAST DUCK

Serves 6–8

1.8 kg/4 lb duck (dressed weight), ask your butcher to bone the duck and cut off the wings at the first joint

salt and pepper

450 g/1 lb flavoured sausage meat, such as Duck & Mango or Pork & Apricot

1 small onion, finely chopped

1 Cox's apple, cored and finely chopped

85 g/3 oz ready-to-eat dried apricots, finely chopped

85 g/3 oz chopped walnuts

2 tbsp chopped fresh parsley

1 large or 2 smaller duck breasts, skin removed

Apricot Sauce (see Accompaniment), to serve

1 Wipe the duck with kitchen paper both inside and out. Lay it skin-side down on a board and season well with salt and pepper.

2 Mix together the sausage meat, onion, apple, apricots, walnuts and parsley and season well with salt and pepper. Form into a large sausage shape.

3 Lay the duck breast(s) on the whole duck and cover with the stuffing. Wrap the whole duck around the filling and tuck in any leg and neck flaps.

4 Preheat the oven to 190°C/375°F/Gas Mark 5.

5 Sew the duck up the back and across both ends with fine string. Try to use one piece of string so that you can remove it in one go. Mould the duck into a good shape and place, sewn-side down, on a wire rack over a roasting tin.

6 Roast for 1½–2 hours, basting occasionally. Pour off some of the fat in the tin. When it is cooked, the duck should be golden brown and crispy.

7 Carve the duck into thick slices at the table and serve with apricot sauce.

ACCOMPANIMENT

Apricot Sauce

Purée 400 g/14 oz canned apricot halves in syrup in a blender. Pour the purée into a saucepan and add 150 ml/5 fl oz stock, 125 ml/4 fl oz Marsala, ½ teaspoon ground cinnamon and ½ teaspoon ground ginger and season with salt and pepper. Stir over a low heat, then simmer for 2–3 minutes. Serve warm.

Turkey is now the favourite Christmas dinner in Britain. Roast turkey, served with all the trimmings, is the seasonal favourite many of us look forward to. There is much debate as to whether it is safe to stuff the bird. Here I give a fruit and vegetable stuffing for the body that is not too dense and also keeps the bird moist, and offer an alternative traditional chestnut stuffing for the neck. One stuffing will suffice, but two is even better and adds more variety to this delicous combination of flavours.

ROAST TURKEY WITH TWO STUFFINGS

Serves 4

4.5 kg/10 lb turkey

salt and pepper

115 g/4 oz butter, softened

10 streaky bacon rashers

for the celery and walnut stuffing

2 onions, finely chopped

2 tbsp butter

55 g/2 oz fresh wholemeal breadcrumbs

4 celery sticks, chopped

2 Cox's apples, cored and roughly chopped

115 g/4 oz dried ready-to-eat apricots, chopped

115 g/4 oz walnuts, chopped

salt and pepper

2 tbsp chopped fresh parsley

for the chestnut stuffing

115 g/4 oz lardons or strips of streaky bacon

1 onion, finely chopped

2 tbsp butter

115 g/4 oz button mushrooms, sliced

225 g/8 oz chestnut purée

2 tbsp chopped fresh parsley

grated rind of 2 lemons

salt and pepper

for the gravy

2 tbsp plain flour

1 litre/1¾ pints stock, if possible made from the giblets

125 ml/4 fl oz red wine or sherry

1 Preheat the oven to 220°C/425°F/Gas Mark 7.

2 Wipe the turkey inside and out with kitchen paper. Season, both inside and out, with salt and pepper.

3 To make the celery and walnut stuffing, fry the onion in the butter in a frying pan until soft. In a bowl, mix together the breadcrumbs, celery, apple, apricots and walnuts. Add the cooked onion and season to taste with salt and pepper. Stir in the parsley.

4 To make the chestnut stuffing, cook the lardons and onion in the butter in a frying pan until soft. Add the mushrooms and cook for 1–2 minutes, then remove from the heat. In a bowl, mix together the chestnut purée with the parsley and lemon rind and season well with salt and pepper. Add the contents of the frying pan to the bowl and mix well. Cool before using to stuff the turkey.

5 Stuff the body cavity of the turkey with the celery and walnut stuffing and the neck with the chestnut stuffing. Secure the neck skin with metal skewers and the legs with string.

6 Cover the bird all over with the butter and squeeze some under the breast skin. Use a little to grease the roasting tin. Place the bird in the tin, season again with salt and pepper and cover the breast with the bacon rashers.

7 Cover the bird with foil and roast in the oven for 30 minutes. Reduce the oven temperature to 180°C/350°F/Gas Mark 4 and continue to cook for 2½–3 hours, basting the turkey every 30 minutes with the pan juices.

8 Forty-five minutes before the end of the cooking time, remove the foil and allow the turkey to brown, basting from time to time. Remove the bacon rashers when crispy and keep warm.

9 Test that the turkey is cooked by piercing the thickest part of the leg with a sharp knife or skewer to make sure the juices run clear. Also, pull a leg slightly away from the body; it should feel loose.

10 Remove the turkey from the roasting tin and place on a warm serving plate, cover with foil and leave to rest whilst you complete the remainder of the meal. Don't worry, you can leave it for up to 1 hour!

11 To make the gravy, drain the fat from the tin and place over a low heat on top of the stove. Sprinkle in the flour, stir well using a small whisk to make a smooth paste and cook for 1 minute. Add the stock a little at a time, whisking constantly, until you have a smooth gravy. Add the wine and bubble together until the gravy is slightly reduced. Season to taste. When you carve the turkey some meat juices will escape: add these to the gravy and stir.

12 Carefully pour the gravy into a warmed serving jug and serve with slices of carved turkey and the spare stuffing spooned into a warm dish.

ACCOMPANIMENTS

Cocktail sausages and bacon rolls are often served with roast turkey, especially at Christmas. Brussels sprouts mixed with some chopped chestnuts are also traditional, as are roast potatoes and parsnips.

Cranberry Sauce

Place 225 g/8 oz fresh cranberries in a saucepan and add 85 g/3 oz soft brown sugar, 150 ml/5 fl oz orange juice, ½ teaspoon ground cinnamon and ½ teaspoon grated nutmeg. Bring to the boil slowly, stirring from time to time. Cook for 8–10 minutes until the cranberries have burst, taking care as they may splash. Put the sauce in a serving bowl and cover until needed. Serve warm or cold with the turkey.

Bread Sauce

Make 12 small holes in a whole peeled onion using a skewer and stick a clove in each hole. Place the onion, 1 bay leaf and 6 peppercorns in a small saucepan and pour in 600 ml/1 pint milk. Place over a medium heat, bring to the boil, remove from the heat, then cover and leave to infuse for 1 hour. Strain the milk and discard the onion, bay leaf and peppercorns. Return the milk to the rinsed-out saucepan and add 115 g/4 oz fresh white breadcrumbs. Cook the sauce over a very gentle heat until the breadcrumbs have swollen and the sauce is thick. Beat in 25 g/1 oz butter and season well with salt and pepper to taste. Add a good grating of fresh nutmeg and stir in 2 tablespoons double cream (optional) before serving. Pour into a warm serving bowl and serve warm with the turkey.

Game is the term given to wild animals and birds that are hunted for the table. Today, however, many of these same animals are farmed or bred especially. The most popular birds are wild duck, pheasant, grouse, partridge, woodcock, pigeon and quail. Game animals include deer (venison), rabbit, hares and wild boars. Take care to remove any shot pellets from game before cooking. For a pie, any meat or combination of meats can be used, although the cooking time will vary according to the type and cut of meat.

GAME PIE

Serves 4–6

oil, for greasing

700 g/1 lb 9 oz mixed game, cut into 3-cm/1¼-inch pieces

2 tbsp plain flour, seasoned with salt and pepper

3 tbsp vegetable oil

1 onion, roughly chopped

1 garlic clove, finely chopped

350 g/12 oz large field mushrooms, sliced

1 tsp crushed juniper berries

125 ml/4 fl oz port or Marsala

450 ml/16 fl oz chicken or game stock

1 bay leaf

400 g/14 oz ready-made puff pastry

1 egg, beaten

1 Preheat the oven to 160°C/325°F/Gas Mark 3. Grease a 1.2-litre/2-pint pie dish. Put the meat and flour in a large plastic bag and shake to coat the meat.

2 Heat the oil in a large casserole dish over a high heat and brown the meat in batches. Remove with a slotted spoon and keep warm. Fry the onion and garlic for 2–3 minutes until softened, then add the mushrooms and cook for about 2 minutes, stirring constantly, until they start to wilt. Add the juniper berries, then the port and scrape the bits from the base of the casserole. Add the stock, stirring constantly, and bring to the boil. Bubble for 2–3 minutes. Add the bay leaf and return the meat to the casserole. Cover and cook in the oven for 1½–2 hours until the meat is tender. Check for seasoning and add more salt and pepper if necessary. Remove from the oven and cool. Chill overnight in the refrigerator to develop the flavours. Remove the bay leaf.

3 Preheat the oven to 200°C/400°F/Gas Mark 6.

4 Roll out the pastry on a lightly floured work surface to about 7 cm/2¾ inches larger than the pie dish. Cut off a 3-cm/1¼-inch strip around the edge. Moisten the rim of the dish and press the pastry strip on to it. Place a pie funnel in the centre of the dish and spoon in the meat filling. Don't overfill; keep any extra gravy to serve separately.

5 Moisten the pastry collar with a little water and put on the pastry lid. Crimp the edges of the pastry firmly and glaze with the egg.

6 Bake the pie on a tray near the top of the oven for about 30 minutes. If necessary, cover it with foil and reduce the oven temperature a little. The pie should be golden brown and the filling bubbling hot.

Coronation Chicken was devised for the Coronation lunch in June 1953 by Rosemary Hume and Constance Spry, co-principals of the Cordon Bleu cookery school. Since then it has become a great standby, often used for summer lunches and weddings. This recipe is made from chicken breasts rather than a whole chicken, and the sauce includes apricots and yogurt. It is an ideal dish for a large number of guests (simply multiply the ingredients) – it is easy to serve and can be accompanied by a selection of salads.

CORONATION CHICKEN

Serves 6

4 boneless chicken breasts
1 bay leaf
1 small onion, sliced
1 carrot, sliced
salt and pepper
4 peppercorns
1 tbsp olive oil
2 shallots, finely chopped
2 tsp mild curry paste
2 tsp tomato purée
juice of ½ lemon
300 ml/10 fl oz mayonnaise
150 ml/5 fl oz natural yogurt
85 g/3 oz ready-to-eat dried apricots, chopped
2 tbsp chopped fresh parsley, to garnish

1 Place the chicken breasts in a large saucepan with the bay leaf, onion and carrot. Cover with water and add ½ teaspoon salt and the peppercorns. Bring to the boil over a medium heat, reduce the heat and simmer very gently for 20–25 minutes. Remove from the heat and allow to cool in the liquor. Reserve 150 ml/½ pint of the stock for the sauce.

2 Meanwhile, heat the oil in a frying pan and sauté the shallots gently for 2–3 minutes until soft but not coloured. Stir in the curry paste and continue to cook for a further minute. Stir in the reserved stock, the tomato purée and the lemon juice and simmer for 10 minutes until the sauce is quite thick. Cool.

3 Remove the chicken from the stock, take off the skin and slice into neat pieces.

4 Mix together the mayonnaise and the yogurt and stir into the sauce. Add the chopped apricots and season to taste with salt and pepper.

5 Stir the chicken into the sauce until well coated and turn into a serving dish. Allow to stand for at least 1 hour for the flavours to mingle. Serve garnished with the chopped parsley.

Shepherd's pie has always been a nursery and school favourite and is classic, feel-good food. It is simple to prepare and can be made ahead and reheated. Traditionally it was put together from leftover lamb from the Sunday joint and served as a family meal in the week. Using good-quality minced lamb gives a much better flavour. Shepherd's pie is often confused with cottage pie, but that version is always made with minced beef rather than lamb.

SHEPHERD'S PIE

Serves 6

1 tbsp olive oil

2 onions, finely chopped

2 garlic cloves, finely chopped

675 g/1½ lb good-quality minced lamb

2 carrots, finely chopped

salt and pepper

1 tbsp plain flour

225 ml/8 fl oz beef or chicken stock

125 ml/4 fl oz red wine

Worcestershire sauce (optional)

for the mashed potato

675 g/1½ lb floury potatoes, such as King Edwards, Maris Piper or Desirée, peeled and cut into chunks

55 g/2 oz butter

2 tbsp cream or milk

salt and pepper

1 Preheat the oven to 180°C/350°F/Gas Mark 4.

2 Heat the oil in a large casserole dish and fry the onion until softened, then add the garlic and stir well.

3 Raise the heat and add the meat. Cook quickly to brown the meat all over, stirring continually. Add the carrot and season well with salt and pepper.

4 Stir in the flour and add the stock and wine. Stir well and heat until simmering and thickened.

5 Cover the casserole dish and cook in the oven for about 1 hour. Check the consistency from time to time and add a little more stock or wine if required. The meat mixture should be quite thick but not dry. Season with salt and pepper to taste and add a little Worcestershire sauce, if desired.

6 While the meat is cooking, make the mashed potato. Cook the potatoes in a large saucepan of boiling salted water for 15–20 minutes. Drain well and mash with a potato masher until smooth. Add the butter and cream and season well with salt and pepper.

7 Spoon the lamb mixture into an ovenproof serving dish and spread or pipe the potato on top.

8 Increase the oven temperature to 200°C/400°F/Gas Mark 6 and cook the pie for 15–20 minutes at the top of the oven until golden brown. You might like to finish it off under a medium grill for a really crisp brown topping to the potato.

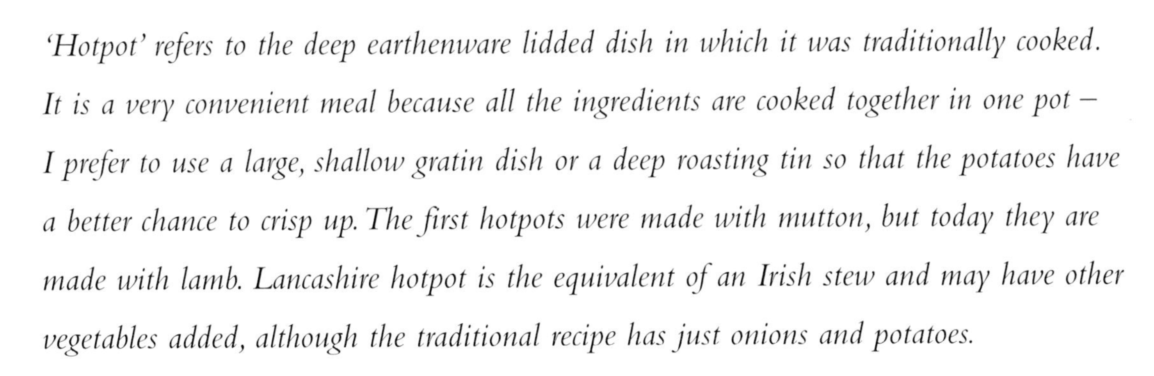

'Hotpot' refers to the deep earthenware lidded dish in which it was traditionally cooked. It is a very convenient meal because all the ingredients are cooked together in one pot – I prefer to use a large, shallow gratin dish or a deep roasting tin so that the potatoes have a better chance to crisp up. The first hotpots were made with mutton, but today they are made with lamb. Lancashire hotpot is the equivalent of an Irish stew and may have other vegetables added, although the traditional recipe has just onions and potatoes.

LANCASHIRE HOTPOT

Serves 4–6

900 g/2 lb best end lamb chops

3 lambs' kidneys

salt and pepper

55 g/2 oz butter

900 g/2 lb floury potatoes, such as King Edwards or Maris Piper, peeled and sliced

3 onions, halved and finely sliced

2 tsp fresh thyme leaves

1 tsp finely chopped fresh rosemary

600 ml/1 pint chicken stock

1 Preheat the oven to 160°C/325°F/Gas Mark 3.

2 Trim the chops of any excess fat. Cut the kidneys in half, remove the core and cut into quarters. Season all the meat well with salt and pepper.

3 Butter a large, shallow ovenproof dish or deep roasting tin with half the butter and arrange a layer of potatoes in the bottom. Layer up the onions and meat, seasoning well with salt and pepper and sprinkling in the herbs between each layer. Finish with a neat layer of overlapping potatoes.

4 Pour in most of the stock so that it covers the meat.

5 Melt the remaining butter and brush the top of the potato with it. Reserve any remaining butter. Cover with foil and cook in the oven for 2 hours.

6 Uncover the hotpot and brush the potatoes again with the melted butter.

7 Return the hotpot to the oven and cook for a further 30 minutes, allowing the potatoes to get brown and crisp. You may need to increase the temperature if not browning sufficiently, or pop under a hot grill.

Cook's tip

Serve the hotpot at the table, making sure that everyone gets a good helping of crusty potato and the meat. Traditionally, hotpot is served with pickled cabbage, but Sweet-&-Sour Red Cabbage (see page 161) would be good too.

This hearty dish is ideal for cold winter months. It is prepared by long slow cooking in a liquid to ensure that the meat is very tender. Originally it made use of tougher, cheaper cuts of meat and, sadly, the poor ingredients gave 'stew' a bad name. Here though, the dish is made with quality ingredients and topped with old-fashioned herb dumplings.

BEEF STEW WITH HERB DUMPLINGS

Serves 6

3 tbsp olive oil

2 onions, finely sliced

2 garlic cloves, chopped

1 kg/2 lb 4 oz good-quality braising steak

2 tbsp plain flour

salt and pepper

300 ml/½ pint beef stock

bouquet garni (bunch of mixed fresh herbs)

150 ml/¼ pint red wine

1 tbsp chopped fresh parsley, to garnish

for the herb dumplings

115 g/4 oz self-raising flour, plus extra for shaping

55 g/2 oz suet

1 tsp mustard

1 tbsp chopped fresh parsley

1 tsp chopped fresh sage

salt and pepper

4 tbsp cold water

1 Preheat the oven to 150°C/300°F/Gas Mark 2.

2 Heat 1 tablespoon of the oil in a large frying pan and fry the onion and garlic until soft and brown. Remove from the pan using a slotted spoon and place in a large casserole dish.

3 Trim the meat and cut into thick strips. Using the remaining oil, fry the meat in the frying pan over a high heat, stirring well until it is brown all over.

4 Sprinkle in the flour and stir well to prevent lumps. Season well.

5 Over a medium heat, pour in the stock, stirring all the time to make a smooth sauce, then continue to heat until boiling.

6 Carefully turn the contents of the frying pan into the casserole dish. Add the bouquet garni and the wine. Cover and cook gently for 2–2½ hours.

7 Start making the dumplings 20 minutes before the stew is ready. Place the dry ingredients, herbs and seasoning in a bowl and mix well. Just before adding the dumplings to the stew, add enough of the water to the mixture to form a firm but soft dough. Break the dough into 12 pieces and roll them into round dumplings (you might need some flour on your hands for this).

8 Remove the stew from the oven, check the seasoning, discard the bouquet garni and add the dumplings, pushing them down under the liquid. Cover and return the dish to the oven, continuing to cook for 15 minutes until the dumplings have doubled in size.

9 Serve piping hot with the parsley scattered over the top.

Steak and kidney steamed in a suet crust pastry, flavoured with mushrooms and parsley, must be the most British of British meat dishes. Also going by the affectionate cockney name of 'Kate & Sydney', this pudding is traditional all over the British Isles. Initially it was made just with steak, but in the 1860s Mrs Beeton published a recipe using steak and kidney, and it has lasted as such up until now. Sometimes oysters were included in the pudding when they were cheap, but are now viewed as too costly.

STEAK & KIDNEY PUDDING

Serves 4

butter, for greasing

450 g/1 lb braising steak, trimmed and cut into 2.5-cm/1-inch pieces

2 lamb's kidneys, cored and cut into 2.5-cm/ 1-inch pieces

55 g/2 oz flour

salt and pepper

1 onion, finely chopped

115 g/4 oz large field mushrooms, sliced (optional)

1 tbsp chopped fresh parsley

300 ml/½ pint (approx) stock, or a mixture of beer and water

for the suet pastry

350 g/12 oz self-raising flour

175 g/6 oz suet

salt and pepper

225 ml/8 fl oz cold water

1 Grease a 1.2-litre/2-pint pudding basin.

2 Put the prepared meat with the flour and salt and pepper into a large plastic bag and shake well until all the meat is well coated. Add the onion, mushrooms, if using, and the parsley and shake again.

3 Make the suet pastry by mixing the flour, suet and some salt and pepper together. Add enough of the cold water to make a soft dough.

4 Keep a quarter of the dough to one side and roll the remainder out to form a circle big enough to line the pudding basin. Line the basin, making sure that there is a good 1 cm/½ inch hanging over the edge.

5 Place the meat mixture in the basin and pour in enough of the stock to cover the meat.

6 Roll out the remaining pastry to make a lid. Fold in the edges of the pastry, dampen them and place the lid on top. Seal firmly in place.

7 Cover with a piece of greaseproof paper and then foil, with a pleat to allow for expansion during cooking, and seal well. Place in a steamer or large saucepan half-filled with boiling water. Simmer the pudding for 4–5 hours, topping up the water from time to time.

8 Remove the basin from the steamer and take off the coverings. Wrap a clean cloth around the basin and serve at the table.

Like steak & kidney pudding (see page 119), this dish also goes by the cockney rhyming slang name of 'Kate & Sydney', and is just as traditional throughout Britain. Some people use shortcrust pastry, but the richer puff pastry is better as it gives a really crisp crust while allowing the base of the pastry to absorb some of the gravy and hence have a better flavour. There are of course regional variations of steak & kidney pie and some cooks add mushrooms and oysters.

STEAK & KIDNEY PIE

Serves 4–6

butter, for greasing

700 g/1 lb 9 oz braising steak, trimmed and cut into 4-cm/1½-inch pieces

3 lambs' kidneys, cored and cut into 2.5-cm/1-inch pieces

2 tbsp plain flour

salt and pepper

3 tbsp vegetable oil

1 onion, roughly chopped

1 garlic clove, finely chopped

125 ml/4 fl oz red wine

450 ml/16 fl oz stock

1 bay leaf

400 g/14 oz ready-made puff pastry

1 egg, beaten

1 Preheat the oven to 160°C/325°F/Gas Mark 3. Grease a 1.2-litre/2-pint pie dish.

2 Put the prepared meat with the flour and salt and pepper in a large plastic bag and shake well until all the meat is well coated.

3 Heat the oil in a flameproof casserole over a high heat and brown the meat in batches. Remove from the casserole with a slotted spoon and keep warm. Fry the onion and garlic in the casserole for 2–3 minutes until softening.

4 Stir in the wine and scrape the base of the pan to release the sediment. Pour in the stock, stirring constantly, and bring to the boil. Bubble for 2–3 minutes. Add the bay leaf and return the meat to the casserole. Cover and cook in the centre of the oven for 1½–2 hours. Check the seasoning, then remove the bay leaf. Leave the meat to cool, preferably overnight, to develop the flavours.

5 Preheat the oven to 200°C/400°F/Gas Mark 6.

6 Roll out the pastry on a lightly floured work surface to about 7 cm/2¾ inches larger than the pie dish. Cut off a 3-cm/1¼-inch strip from the edge. Moisten the rim of the dish and press the pastry strip onto it. Place the pie funnel in the centre of the dish and spoon in the steak and kidney filling. Don't overfill, keeping any extra gravy to serve separately. Moisten the pastry collar with water and put on the pastry lid, taking care to fit it carefully around the pie funnel. Crimp the edges of the pastry firmly and glaze with the egg.

7 Place the pie on a tray towards the top of the oven for about 30 minutes. The pie should be golden brown and the filling bubbling hot; cover it with foil and reduce the temperature if the pastry is getting too brown.

Pork fillet or tenderloin is the tenderest part of the pig. It is very lean and can be sliced and cooked as escalopes or, as here, stuffed and sliced before serving. You can choose any stuffing, but this one using Lancashire cheese is a favourite from my childhood. The use of cider is also traditional – the combination of apples with pork goes back to the time when pigs were kept in farm orchards and allowed to eat the windfall apples: perhaps the apple flavour was apparent in the meat.

LANCASHIRE CHEESE-STUFFED PORK FILLET

Serves 4

2 pork fillets, weighing 350 g/12 oz each

salt and pepper

2 thin slices of cooked ham (or use Parma ham)

85 g/3 oz Lancashire cheese, crumbled

4 ready-to-eat prunes, cut in half

4 fresh sage leaves, chopped

25 g/1 oz butter

225 ml/8 fl oz cider or apple juice

1 tsp mild mustard

125 ml/4 fl oz single cream

1 Preheat the oven to 190°C/375°F/Gas Mark 5.

2 Cut the fillets down the centre, but do not cut right through. Spread them open and flatten out. You can bash the fillets with a rolling pin to flatten them out more if you wish.

3 Season the fillets well with salt and pepper and place a piece of ham on each one. Crumble over the cheese and arrange the prunes in between. Sprinkle over the sage leaves.

4 Fold the fillets over into neat sausage shapes and secure with cocktail sticks or tie with string to make sure they keep their shape.

5 Place in a small roasting tin, dot with the butter and pour over the cider.

6 Cover with foil and cook in the oven for 40–45 minutes, removing the foil for the last 10 minutes.

7 Remove the tin from the oven and place the pork on a warm plate. Remove the cocktail sticks or string and allow to rest for 10 minutes in a warm place.

8 Place the roasting tin on the stove over a medium heat and stir the juices well to mix. Add the mustard and bubble away until the sauce is quite thick. Stir in the cream and heat through.

9 Slice the pork across diagonally and serve the sauce separately.

I remember toad in the hole as our favourite Saturday lunch, though I never knew where the name came from and in fact no one seems to have a reliable answer. Batter puddings are known in many regions and this dish is really just Yorkshire pudding batter cooked around sausages. Although a modest meal, it can be really satisfying, particularly if you take advantage of the wide range of good, well-flavoured sausages available today.

TOAD IN THE HOLE

Serves 4

oil, for greasing

115 g/4 oz plain flour

pinch of salt

1 egg, beaten

300 ml/½ pint milk

450 g/1 lb good-quality pork sausages

1 tbsp vegetable oil

1 Grease a 20 x 25-cm/8 x 10-inch ovenproof dish or roasting tin.

2 Make the batter by sifting the flour and salt into a mixing bowl. Make a well in the centre and add the beaten egg and half the milk. Carefully stir the liquid into the flour until the mixture is smooth. Gradually beat in the remaining milk. Leave to stand for 30 minutes.

3 Preheat the oven to 220°C/425°F/Gas Mark 7.

4 Prick the sausages and place them in the dish. Sprinkle over the oil and cook the sausages in the oven for 10 minutes until they are beginning to colour and the fat has started to run and is sizzling.

5 Remove from the oven and quickly pour the batter over the sausages. Return to the oven and cook for 35–45 minutes until the toad is well risen and golden brown. Serve immediately.

Cook's tip

Toad in the hole is delicious served with Onion Gravy (see page 128) or just a pile of softly fried onions.

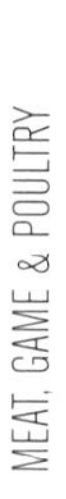

Cornish pasties were made by women for their menfolk to take down the tin mines. The pastry shape was a convenient one to put in the pocket. Sometimes the pasties had meat at one end and fruit at the other to make a complete meal. The filling is a mixture of beef, onions, potato and swede (sometimes known as turnip in Cornwall). Today, they are still popular throughout the West Country and are particularly good eaten hot from the oven in winter after a long exhausting walk.

CORNISH PASTIES

Serves 4

250 g/9 oz chuck steak, trimmed and cut into 1-cm/½-inch dice

175 g/6 oz swede, peeled and cut into 1-cm/½-inch dice

350 g/12 oz potatoes, peeled and cut into 1-cm/½-inch dice

1 onion, finely chopped

salt and pepper

1 egg, beaten

for the shortcrust pastry

450 g/1 lb plain flour, plus extra for dusting

pinch of salt

115 g/4 oz lard

115 g/4 oz butter

175 ml/6 fl oz cold water

1 To make the pastry, sift the flour and salt into a bowl and gently rub in the lard and butter until the mixture resembles breadcrumbs. Add the water, a spoonful at a time, and stir the mixture with a knife until it holds together.

2 Turn out onto a lightly floured surface and gently press together until smooth. Wrap in clingfilm and allow to chill for 1 hour.

3 Meanwhile, to prepare the filling, mix the meat and vegetables together and season well with salt and pepper.

4 Divide the pastry into 4 even-sized pieces and roll one out until just larger than the size of a 20-cm/8-inch plate. Place the plate on top of the pastry and cut round it to give a neat edge. Repeat with the other pieces.

5 Arrange the meat and vegetable mixture across the 4 rounds of pastry, making sure the filling goes to the edge.

6 Brush the edges of the pastry with water, then bring the edges up over the filling and press together to form a ridge. You can flute the edges of the pasties with your fingers or fold over the pastry to form a cord-like seal. Tuck in the ends.

7 Allow to chill for 1 hour, then glaze with the egg.

8 Preheat the oven to 190°C/375°F/Gas Mark 5.

9 Place on a greased baking tray and cook in the centre of the oven for 50–60 minutes. The pasties should be crisp and golden in colour. Cover with foil and reduce the temperature if the pastry is getting too brown.

Bangers & Mash must be many people's idea of heaven. If you buy good-quality wonderfully flavoured sausages, make perfect mash and add a truly rich onion gravy, this is a dish fit for angels. We all have our favourite sausages, be they plain pork, Cumberland, or more unusual varieties like venison. Fry them thoroughly to ensure the insides are cooked and the skin is so crisp and sticky that it almost sticks to the frying pan, or put them in the oven at 180°C/350°F/Gas Mark 4 for 25–30 minutes.

SAUSAGES & MASH WITH ONION GRAVY

Serves 4

8 good-quality sausages

1 tbsp oil

for the onion gravy

3 onions, cut in half and thinly sliced

70 g/2½ oz butter

125 ml/4 fl oz Marsala or port

125 ml/4 fl oz vegetable stock

salt and pepper

for the mashed potato

900 g/2 lb floury potatoes, such as King Edwards, Maris Piper or Desirée, peeled and cut into chunks

salt and pepper

55 g/2 oz butter

3 tbsp hot milk

2 tbsp chopped fresh parsley

1 Cook the sausages slowly in a frying pan with the oil over a low heat. Cover the pan and turn the sausages from time to time. Don't rush the cooking, because you want them well-cooked and sticky. They will take 25–30 minutes.

2 Meanwhile, prepare the onion gravy by placing the onion in a frying pan with the butter and frying over a low heat until soft, stirring continuously. Continue to cook until they are brown and almost melting, stirring from time to time. This will take about 30 minutes, but it is worth it as the onions will naturally caramelize.

3 Pour in the Marsala and stock and continue to bubble away until the onion gravy is really thick. Season with salt and pepper to taste.

4 To make the mashed potato, cook the potatoes in a large saucepan of boiling salted water for 15–20 minutes. Drain well and mash with a potato masher until smooth. Season with salt and pepper, add the butter, milk and parsley and stir well.

5 Serve the sausages really hot with the mashed potato and the onion gravy spooned over the top.

Venison is a very British meat, particularly well known in Scotland. It was traditionally meat from hunted wild deer, the season being from late June to January, but now it is available farmed all year round. Today venison is being eaten more and more because it is a healthy meat due to its relatively low fat and cholesterol content. It tends to be a dry meat, though, so it is best to casserole it to ensure it is tender.

VENISON CASSEROLE

Serves 4–6

- 3 tbsp olive oil
- 1 kg/2 lb 4 oz casserole venison, cut into 3-cm/1¼-inch cubes
- 2 onions, finely sliced
- 2 garlic cloves, chopped
- 2 tbsp plain flour
- 350 ml/12 fl oz beef or vegetable stock
- 125 ml/4 fl oz port or red wine
- 2 tbsp redcurrant jelly
- 6 crushed juniper berries
- pinch of ground cinnamon
- whole nutmeg, for grating
- 175 g/6 oz vacuum-packed chestnuts (optional)
- salt and pepper

1 Preheat the oven to 150°C/300°F/Gas Mark 2.

2 Heat the oil in a large frying pan and brown the cubes of venison over a high heat. You may need to fry the meat in 2 or 3 batches – do not overcrowd the frying pan. Remove the venison using a slotted spoon and place in a large casserole dish.

3 Add the onion and garlic to the frying pan and fry until a good golden colour, then add to the meat. Sprinkle the meat in the casserole dish with the flour and turn to coat evenly.

4 Gradually add the stock to the frying pan, stir well and scrape up the sediment, then bring to the boil. Add to the casserole dish and stir well, ensuring that the meat is just covered.

5 Add the port, redcurrant jelly, juniper berries, cinnamon, a small grating of nutmeg and the chestnuts, if using. Season well with the salt and pepper, cover and cook gently in the centre of the oven for 2–2½ hours.

6 Remove from the oven and season with more salt and pepper if necessary. Serve immediately, piping hot.

Cook's tip

This casserole benefits from being made the day before to allow the flavours to develop. Reheat gently before serving. Ensure you cool the casserole as quickly as possible and store in the refrigerator or a cool larder overnight. Serve the casserole with baked or mashed potatoes.

5

VEGETABLES & SALADS

Vegetables have had a chequered history in British cooking. Hundreds of years ago they were revered both in culinary and medicinal terms, particularly all the salad leaves and herbs, and were eaten raw. It is the Romans who are credited with bringing about 200 varieties of Mediterranean herbs to Britain, and the widely available salad leaves and herbs we use today are just like the ones eaten in those far off times. After the Romans left Britain, vegetables were not seen as something to eat fresh or in their own right. Instead, they were regarded as fit only to be cooked for a long time to produce the thick soups and stews that were the staple food of the poor. Perhaps this is where we get our reputation for overcooking vegetables. Now, thankfully, we eat them on their own or as accompaniments to meat or fish.

During the seventeenth and eighteenth centuries, wealthy country landowners spent huge amounts of money on their gardens and farms, and fruit and vegetable growing became very popular as a means of providing food for their tables. In the towns, however, meat was established as such a desirable food item that vegetables were rarely on the menu. It was only when country gardeners established market gardens and their produce started to be transported to the towns that vegetables began to be used in their own right. Cookery books of the day also started to list recipes for vegetables separately from meat dishes.

The Victorians changed the prevailing attitude. They thought that vegetables were good for you and served them separately at dinner, perhaps one or two together with potatoes. This habit continued in Britain largely until the 1960s, when there was a big interest in vegetarianism prompted by people's dislike of factory farming and the way animals were killed. By the 1970s, it was not unusual at dinner parties to be served with a platter of six or seven different vegetables. This also reflected the fact that some people were trying to be self-sufficient and grow all their own vegetables, either in their gardens or on allotments. I remember shelling fresh peas, topping Brussels sprouts and destringing runner beans – all taken straight from the garden. The vegetables were harvested while still young and cooked for a short time only, so that they retained their 'bite'. A plate of these vegetables served with a little butter and a sprinkling of sea salt was a meal in itself. In the 1960s and 1970s, the first vegetarians were regarded as rather eccentric and were called the 'beard and sandal brigade', but today there are more vegetarians in Britain than ever before, mostly choosing what they believe to be a healthier option.

Currently we have excellent sources of fresh salads and vegetables. Supermarkets have been leaders in supplying a real choice of leaves – watercress, lamb's lettuce, mizuna, rocket, Swiss chard, radicchio and sorrel – washed and ready to serve from the bag. Freshly picked and growing herbs mean we have a year-round supply of parsley, basil, coriander, chives, rosemary, mint and thyme. Both fresh and frozen produce sourced from all over the world give us a suberb selection of prepared fruit, vegetables and herbs, particularly during the winter months.

Many producers are growing vegetables and salads organically and these are certified by The Soil Association. The flavours of these vegetables can be very good and you are assured that they are grown without the use of pesticides and extra fertilizers.

Fresh asparagus is considered a delicacy due to its relatively short season: May to early July. It has been grown in Britain for centuries, particularly in the Vale of Evesham. It is labour-intensive to produce and its growing habit means that the plants are only productive for half their lives. We eat green asparagus, but in France and Belgium the white variety is more valued. Asparagus can be steamed, boiled, grilled or roasted, and served simply with butter or hollandaise sauce as a starter and eaten using fingers.

ASPARAGUS WITH MELTED BUTTER

Serves 2

16–20 stalks of asparagus, trimmed to about 20 cm/8 inches

85 g/3 oz unsalted butter, melted

sea salt and pepper, to serve

1 Remove some of the base of the asparagus stalks with a potato peeler if they are rather thick.

2 Tie the stalks together with string or use a wire basket so that they can easily be removed from the pan without damage.

3 Bring a large saucepan of salted water to the boil and plunge in the stalks. Cover with a lid and cook for 4–5 minutes. Pierce one stalk near the base with a sharp knife. If it is fairly soft remove from the heat at once. Do not overcook asparagus or the tender tips will fall off.

4 Drain the asparagus thoroughly and serve on large warm plates with the butter poured over. Both the butter and the asparagus should be warm rather than hot. Serve with the salt and pepper and hand out large napkins!

VARIATIONS

To griddle asparagus, brush a griddle with oil and then heat until it is very hot. Place the asparagus on the griddle and cook for 2 minutes on one side, then turn over and griddle for a further 2 minutes. Serve immediately. Asparagus is also delicious served with hollandaise sauce (see page 77), slices of Parma ham, shavings of Parmesan cheese or soft-boiled quail eggs. Alternatively, fry 55 g/2 oz fresh white breadcrumbs in 40 g/1½ oz butter until golden and crisp and serve scattered over lightly cooked asparagus.

This is the English way of using up leftover potatoes and vegetables, with similar recipes coming from Ireland and Scotland. These filling dishes come from a time when careful housewives made sure they used up all their leftovers. This recipe can also be made from fresh potatoes and cabbage and is all the more delicious for it. You can use sliced potatoes, but mashed is best because it results in a large soft cake. The name of the dish comes from the bubbling sound of the potato in the fat and the squeak of the cabbage.

BUBBLE & SQUEAK

Serves 2–3

450 g/1 lb green cabbage

1 onion, thinly sliced

4 tbsp olive oil

salt and pepper

for the mashed potato

450 g/1 lb floury potatoes, such as King Edwards, Maris Piper or Desirée, peeled and cut into chunks

salt and pepper

55 g/2 oz butter

3 tbsp hot milk

1 To make the mashed potato, cook the potatoes in a large saucepan of boiling salted water for 15–20 minutes. Drain well and mash with a potato masher until smooth. Season with salt and pepper, add the butter and milk and stir well.

2 Cut the cabbage into quarters, remove the centre stalk and shred finely.

3 In a large frying pan, fry the onion in half the oil until soft. Add the cabbage to the pan and stir-fry for 2–3 minutes until softened. Season with salt and pepper, add the mashed potato and mix together well.

4 Press the mixture firmly into the frying pan and allow to cook over a high heat for 4–5 minutes so that the base is crispy. Place a plate over the frying pan and invert the pan so that the potato cake falls onto the plate. Add the remaining oil to the pan, reheat and slip the cake back into the pan with the uncooked side down.

5 Continue to cook for a further 5 minutes until the bottom is crispy too. Turn out onto a hot plate and cut into wedges for serving. Serve at once.

VARIATIONS

This dish can be made with curly kale or Brussels sprouts instead of the cabbage. The potato and cabbage mix can also be formed into small cakes and fried separately like fish cakes. This is a good way for children to be encouraged to eat cabbage. They can also be fried with bacon to accompany bacon and eggs for breakfast.

This tasty dish, from Scotland, is traditionally served with haggis on Burns Night. There is always a great debate amongst cooks as to whether 'neeps' are turnips or swedes. Turnips are white root vegetables and swedes are the larger orange-coloured ones. Most recipes are interchangeable, but for this one I find the coloured swedes are better. 'Bashed neeps' are mashed swedes and are mixed with mashed potato to make the neeps and tatties.

NEEPS & TATTIES

Serves 4–5

450 g/1 lb swedes, peeled and diced

250 g/9 oz floury potatoes, such as King Edwards, Maris Piper or Desirée, peeled and diced

salt and pepper

55 g/2 oz butter

whole nutmeg, for grating

fresh parsley sprigs, to garnish

1 Cook the swede and potato in a large saucepan of boiling salted water for 20 minutes until soft. Test with the point of a knife and if not cooked return to the heat for a further 5 minutes.

2 Drain well, return to the rinsed-out pan and heat for a few moments to ensure they are dry. Mash using a potato masher until smooth. Season well with the salt and pepper and add the butter. Grate as much of the nutmeg into the mash as you like and serve piping hot, garnished with the parsley.

Perfect roast potatoes are crisp on the outside and soft and fluffy on the inside. Do choose the right potatoes – floury ones are best. The choice of fat is also important – goose or duck fat gives an amazing flavour. However, the fat from a joint is almost as good and really tasty potatoes can also be made using olive oil. Parboiling the potatoes is a chore but worthwhile because it gives crusty outsides. A heavy roasting tin will ensure the potatoes don't stick, and a hot oven means they crisp, not steam, in the fat.

PERFECT ROAST POTATOES

Serves 6

1.3 kg/3 lb large floury potatoes, such as King Edwards, Maris Piper or Desirée, peeled and cut into even-sized chunks

salt

3 tbsp dripping, goose fat, duck fat or olive oil

1 Preheat the oven to 220°C/425°F/Gas Mark 7.

2 Cook the potatoes in a large saucepan of boiling salted water over a medium heat, covered, for 5–7 minutes. They will still be firm. Remove from the heat.

3 Meanwhile, add the fat to a roasting tin and place in the hot oven.

4 Drain the potatoes well and return them to the saucepan. Cover with the lid and firmly shake the pan so that the surface of the potatoes is roughened to help give a much crisper texture.

5 Remove the roasting tin from the oven and carefully tip the potatoes into the hot oil. Baste them to ensure they are all coated with the oil.

6 Roast at the top of the oven for 45–50 minutes until they are browned all over and thoroughly crisp. Turn the potatoes and baste again only once during the process or the crunchy edges will be destroyed.

7 Carefully transfer the potatoes from the roasting tin into a hot serving dish. Sprinkle with a little salt and serve at once. Any leftovers (although this is most unlikely) are delicious cold.

VARIATION

Small whole unpeeled new potatoes are delicious roasted too. They don't need any parboiling – just coat them with the hot fat and then roast for 30–40 minutes. Drain well and season with salt and pepper before serving.

Mashed potato is Britain's most long-standing comfort food – almost everyone loves smooth, creamy mashed potato. But it has to be smooth and creamy, not lumpy. Using the right potato is essential – you need floury potatoes such as King Edwards or a good all-rounder like the Desirée. A potato masher is invaluable but I prefer a potato ricer, which presses the potato through tiny holes and makes fine 'worms' which means you never get lumps.

PERFECT MASH

Serves 4

900 g/2 lb floury potatoes, such as King Edwards, Maris Piper or Desirée

55 g/2 oz butter

3 tbsp hot milk

salt and pepper

1 Peel the potatoes, placing them in cold water as you prepare the others to prevent them from going brown.

2 Cut the potatoes into even-sized chunks and cook in a large saucepan of boiling salted water over a medium heat, covered, for 20–25 minutes until they are tender. Test with the point of a knife, but do make sure you test right to the middle to avoid lumps.

3 Remove the pan from the heat and drain the potatoes. Return the potatoes to the hot pan and mash with a potato masher until smooth.

4 Add the butter and continue to mash until it is all mixed in, then add the milk (it is better hot because the potatoes absorb it more quickly to produce a creamier mash).

5 Taste the mash and season with salt and pepper as necessary. Serve at once.

VARIATIONS

For herb mash, mix in 3 tablespoons chopped fresh parsley, thyme or mint. For mustard or horseradish mash, mix in 2 tablespoons wholegrain mustard or horseradish sauce. For pesto mash, stir in 4 tablespoons fresh pesto and for nutmeg mash, grate ½ a nutmeg into the mash and add 125 ml/4 fl oz natural yogurt. To make creamed potato, add 125 ml/4 fl oz soured cream and 2 tablespoons snipped fresh chives.

Potatoes have always been the staple food of Ireland and have been made into many great dishes. Cabbage and kale are also common ingredients and are mixed together in many recipes. Colcannon is a traditional Irish dish often served at Hallowe'en, when lucky charms would be hidden in the mixture (rather like in a Christmas pudding) and those who found them might expect a proposal of marriage. Leeks or spring onions are often added as a variation.

COLCANNON

Serves 3–4

225 g/8 oz green or white cabbage

6 spring onions, cut into 5-mm/¼-inch pieces

salt and pepper

55 g/2 oz butter, cut into 4 pieces

for the mashed potato

450 g/1 lb floury potatoes, such as King Edwards, Maris Piper or Desirée, peeled and cut into chunks

salt and pepper

55 g/2 oz butter

150 ml/5 fl oz single cream

1 To make the mashed potato, cook the potatoes in a large saucepan of boiling salted water for 15–20 minutes. Drain well and mash with a potato masher until smooth. Season with salt and pepper, add the butter and cream and stir well. The potato should be very soft.

2 Cut the cabbage into quarters, remove the centre stalk and shred finely.

3 Cook the cabbage in a large saucepan of boiling salted water for just 1–2 minutes until it is soft. Drain thoroughly.

4 Mix the potato and cabbage together and stir in the spring onion. Season well with salt and pepper.

5 Serve in individual bowls and top with a good piece of butter.

VARIATIONS

This is a totally vegetarian dish and can be eaten on its own or with some grated cheese added. It is also delicious served with cold sliced meats or hot sausages and crisply fried lardons of bacon can be added to give more flavour.

Laver bread is not bread at all, but a dense purée of laver – an edible seaweed that is greatly prized in Wales, particularly in Cardiff and Swansea. It is the same seaweed as nori, which is so highly regarded in Japan. It is available cooked from fishmongers or you can gather your own on the west coast of Wales, if you know what to look for. Laver is usually fried with oatmeal, or can be made into a sauce to serve with lamb. Laver bread is very nutritious, containing protein, carbohydrate, minerals, vitamins and trace elements.

LAVER BREAD

Serves 4

4 tbsp prepared laver

2 tbsp fine oatmeal

2 tbsp bacon fat or vegetable oil

to serve

8 bacon rashers

4 tomatoes, halved

drizzle of oil

salt and pepper

1 Mix the laver with enough oatmeal to make it sufficiently firm to allow you to shape the mixture into 4 small round cakes.

2 Place the bacon rashers in a dry frying pan and fry for 2–4 minutes on each side, depending on how crisp you like your bacon. Remove from the frying pan, leaving all the excess bacon fat, and keep the bacon warm. The frying pan can then be used to fry the laver bread. Heat the bacon fat or oil in the frying pan and fry the laver bread cakes for 4–5 minutes until nicely browned on 1 side. Turn over and repeat until cooked through.

3 Meanwhile, the tomato halves can be placed under a hot grill. Drizzle with a little oil and season to taste with salt and pepper before grilling for 3–4 minutes.

4 Serve the laver bread with the fried bacon and grilled tomatoes.

VARIATIONS

Laver Bread Sauce

Heat 225 g/8 oz laver bread with the juice and grated rind of 1 orange. Season with salt and pepper and add a little lemon juice, to taste. Serve with Welsh roast lamb. A thicker purée of this can also be made to serve as a vegetable with the lamb. Double the quantity of laver bread and add 55 g/2 oz butter. Laver bread sauce can also be served with fish, particularly fresh, wild salmon.

'Pease pudding hot, pease pudding cold, pease pudding in the pot, nine days old' refers to a pudding of dried split peas which keeps well. The British have always preferred peas over other pulses and this dish was popular with poor and rich alike. Originally an accompaniment to boiled ham or bacon, the pudding was boiled in a cloth with the ham. Today it is easily made with a few extra flavourings and steamed in a pudding basin. Eat it freshly made, or serve sliced and fried on subsequent days with cold meats.

PEASE PUDDING

Serves 4–6

350 g/12 oz dried split green peas

1 carrot, finely diced (optional)

1 celery stick, finely diced (optional)

1 onion, finely chopped (optional)

2 tsp vegetable stock powder

salt and pepper

55 g/2 oz butter

1 tbsp chopped fresh mixed herbs

1 egg, beaten

boiled ham or gammon, to serve

1 Wash the peas well. Some dried varieties require soaking – follow directions provided on the pack.

2 Drain the peas, place in a saucepan and cover with fresh water. Place the saucepan over a medium heat and bring to the boil. Add the vegetables, if using, and the stock powder. If you have any meat bones, you could add these. Cook gently for 30–45 minutes until the peas are tender.

3 Remove from the heat and drain off the liquid (this can be retained to make soup) and remove any bones.

4 Purée the pea mixture using a mouli sieve or a food processor. Season well with salt and pepper and beat in the butter, herbs and the egg.

5 Spoon the mixture into a greased 600 ml/1 pint pudding basin, cover with greaseproof paper and foil and steam for 1 hour. Turn out the pudding and serve with boiled ham or gammon.

VARIATION

Mushy Peas

Put 450 g/1 lb whole dried peas into a saucepan with 1 finely chopped onion, 1 finely chopped carrot and a small bunch of mixed fresh herbs. Cover with water, bring to the boil very slowly and simmer very gently for 2 hours. Strain the peas, discard the herbs and mash the peas and vegetables with a potato masher. Add 55 g/2 oz butter, beat into the mixture and season well with salt and pepper. Serve hot with duck, pork or fish and chips.

Tele-Video

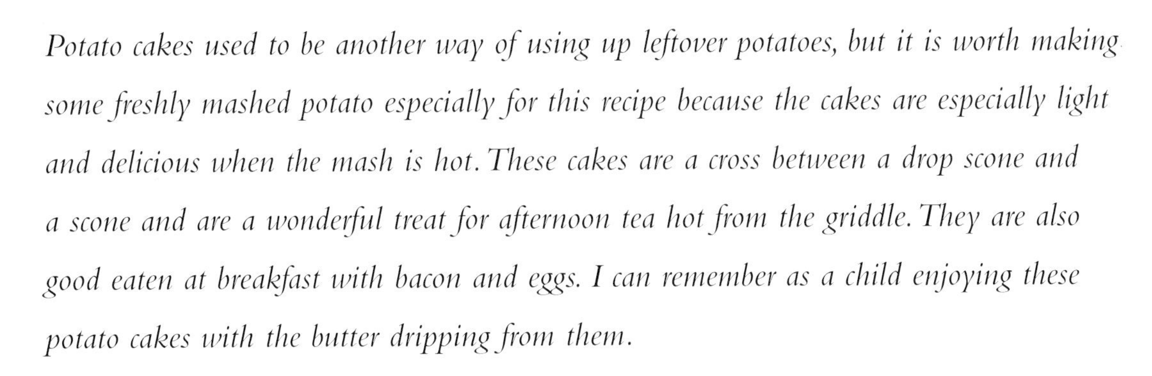

Potato cakes used to be another way of using up leftover potatoes, but it is worth making some freshly mashed potato especially for this recipe because the cakes are especially light and delicious when the mash is hot. These cakes are a cross between a drop scone and a scone and are a wonderful treat for afternoon tea hot from the griddle. They are also good eaten at breakfast with bacon and eggs. I can remember as a child enjoying these potato cakes with the butter dripping from them.

POTATO CAKES

Serves 8–10

550 g/1 lb 4 oz floury potatoes, such as King Edwards, Maris Piper or Desirée, peeled and cut into chunks

25 g/1 oz butter, plus extra to serve

salt and pepper

1 egg (optional)

115 g/4 oz plain flour

1 To make the mashed potato, cook the potatoes in a large saucepan of boiling salted water for 15–20 minutes. Drain well and mash with a potato masher until smooth. Season with salt and pepper and add the butter. Mix in the egg, if using.

2 Turn the mixture out into a large mixing bowl and add enough of the flour to make a light dough. Work quickly as you do not want the potato to cool too much.

3 Place the dough on a lightly floured surface and roll out carefully to a thickness of 5 mm/¼ inch. Using a 6-cm/2½-inch pastry cutter, cut into potato cakes.

4 Heat a greased griddle or heavy-based frying pan. Slip the cakes onto the griddle in batches and cook for 4–5 minutes on each side until they are golden brown.

5 Keep warm on a hot plate and serve immediately with lots of fresh butter.

VARIATION

For a more substantial supper dish for 3–4 people, you could make the potato cakes with a little chopped bacon and sautéed onion. Make the cakes thicker and fry in a mixture of oil and butter for 3–4 minutes on each side. Turn only once to avoid breaking the cakes. Serve hot with a green salad.

Onions form an important part of savoury cooking. Chopped or sliced and fried, they are the base of all casserole dishes and many soup recipes. But cooked on their own, they can be a meal in themselves and are very healthy. Onions are easy to grow and are now found all over the British Isles, but I still remember the 'onion men' from Brittany who used to travel across to Britain with their strings of onions on their bicycles. Sadly this selling practice has all but ceased.

ROASTED ONIONS

Serves 4

8 large onions, peeled

3 tbsp olive oil

55 g/2 oz butter

2 tsp chopped fresh thyme

salt and pepper

200 g/7 oz Cheddar or Lancashire cheese, grated

to serve

salad

crusty bread

1 Preheat the oven to 180°C/350°F/Gas Mark 4.

2 Cut a cross down through the top of the onions towards the root, without cutting all the way through.

3 Place the onions in a roasting tin and drizzle over the olive oil.

4 Press a little of the butter into the open crosses, sprinkle with the thyme and season with salt and pepper. Cover with foil and roast for 40–45 minutes.

5 Remove from the oven, take off the foil and baste the onions with the pan juices. Return to the oven and cook for a further 15 minutes, uncovered, to allow the onions to brown.

6 Take the onions out of the oven and scatter the grated cheese over them. Return them to the oven for a few minutes so that the cheese starts to melt.

7 Serve at once with some salad and lots of warm crusty bread.

VARIATION

Stuffed Onions

Preheat the oven to 220°C/425°F/Gas Mark 7. Peel 4 onions and boil in salted water for 20 minutes. Scoop out the centres of the onions and stuff with a mixture of 55 g/2 oz each of grated cheese and breadcrumbs and 1 teaspoon mustard. Place the stuffed onions in a baking dish, top with 25 g/1 oz butter and bake in the oven for 25–30 minutes. Serve hot as a starter or as an accompaniment to roast meat.

Root vegetables are our winter staples. They keep well and can be cooked in various ways. Roast root vegetables are particularly popular since they all cook together and need little attention once prepared. You can use whatever is available: potatoes, parsnips, turnips, swedes, carrots and, though not strictly root vegetables, squash and onions. Try to have all the vegetables cut to roughly the same size. I always like to use a good handful of herbs, particularly a mixture of the stronger flavoured ones like rosemary, thyme and sage.

ROASTED ROOT VEGETABLES

Serves 4–6

3 parsnips, peeled and cut into 5-cm/2-inch pieces

4 baby turnips, quartered

3 carrots, peeled and cut into 5-cm/2-inch pieces

450 g/1 lb butternut squash, peeled and cut into 5-cm/2-inch chunks

450 g/1 lb sweet potato, peeled and cut into 5-cm/2-inch chunks

2 garlic cloves, finely chopped

2 tbsp chopped fresh rosemary

2 tbsp chopped fresh thyme

2 tsp chopped fresh sage

3 tbsp olive oil

salt and pepper

2 tbsp chopped fresh mixed herbs, such as parsley, thyme and mint, to garnish

1 Preheat the oven to 220°C/425°F/Gas Mark 7.

2 Arrange all the vegetables in a single layer in a large roasting tin. Scatter over the garlic and the herbs.

3 Pour over the oil and season well with the salt and pepper.

4 Toss all the ingredients together until they are well mixed and coated with the oil (you can leave them to marinate at this stage to allow the flavours to be absorbed).

5 Roast at the top of the oven for 50–60 minutes until the vegetables are cooked and nicely browned. Turn the vegetables over halfway through the cooking time.

6 Serve with a good handful of fresh herbs scattered on top and a final sprinkling of salt and pepper.

VARIATIONS

Shallots or wedges of red onion can be added to the root vegetables to give additional flavour and texture. Whole cloves of unpeeled garlic are also good roasted with the other vegetables. You can then squeeze out the creamy cooked garlic over the vegetables when eating them.

This homey pancake dish made from sliced potatoes, onions and cheese, hails from northeast England. Enjoy it as a vegetarian dish with a fresh salad or serve as an accompaniment to grilled meat or fish. One-dish meals are a modern way of providing a quick mid-week supper and are easy to prepare with little washing up afterwards. As a variation, crisply fried pieces of bacon or chunks of cooked ham can be added to give a more substantial meal.

PAN HAGGERTY

Serves 4–5

4 tbsp olive oil

55 g/2 oz butter

450 g/1 lb firm potatoes, Desirée or waxy salad potatoes

225 g/8 oz onions, halved and thinly sliced

115 g/4 oz Cheddar cheese, grated

salt and pepper

1 Heat half the olive oil and half the butter in a 23–25-cm/9–10-inch frying pan.

2 Peel the potatoes if necessary (you don't need to peel small salad potatoes). Slice thinly using a mandolin or food processor. Rinse the slices quickly in cold water and dry thoroughly using a tea towel or kitchen paper.

3 Remove the oil and butter from the heat and arrange the sliced potato in the base of the pan. Build up layers of potato, onion and cheese, seasoning well with salt and pepper between each layer. Finish with a layer of potato and dot the remaining butter over the top.

4 Return to the heat and cook over a medium heat for 15–20 minutes. The base should become brown but not burn. Place a large plate over the frying pan and invert the potato onto the plate by tilting the frying pan. Add the remaining oil to the frying pan and slip the potato back in, cooking the other side for a further 15 minutes until the bottom is crusty.

5 Remove from the heat and serve at once on a warm plate.

Cook's tip

If preferred, the dish can be made in a shallow 25-cm/10-inch gratin dish and cooked in the top of the oven at 180°C/350°F/Gas Mark 4 for 45–50 minutes until piping hot and golden brown.

Cabbage was known in the time of the ancient Egyptians, but only in the last century have we had so many varieties available in Britain. Most people can remember when it was served overcooked at school, but luckily we now cook cabbage for shorter times and without so much water. Red cabbage can be eaten raw and made into coleslaw, but it is best when cooked with apples and wine vinegar and flavoured with spices and redcurrant jelly – a sort of 'sweet-and-sour' dish.

SWEET-&-SOUR RED CABBAGE

Serves 6–8

- 1 red cabbage, about 750 g/1 lb 10 oz
- 2 tbsp olive oil
- 2 onions, finely sliced
- 1 garlic clove, chopped
- 2 small cooking apples, peeled, cored and sliced
- 2 tbsp muscovado sugar
- ½ tsp ground cinnamon
- 1 tsp crushed juniper berries
- whole nutmeg, for grating
- 2 tbsp red wine vinegar
- grated rind and juice of 1 orange
- salt and pepper
- 2 tbsp redcurrant jelly

1 Cut the cabbage into quarters, remove the centre stalk and shred finely.

2 Pour the oil into a large saucepan and add the red cabbage, onion, garlic and apple.

3 Sprinkle on the sugar, cinnamon and juniper berries and grate a quarter of the nutmeg into the pan.

4 Pour over the red wine vinegar and orange juice and add the orange rind.

5 Stir well and season with the salt and pepper. The saucepan will be quite full but the volume of the cabbage will reduce during cooking.

6 Cook over medium heat, stirring well from time to time, until the cabbage is just tender but still has 'bite'. This will take 10–15 minutes depending on how finely the cabbage is sliced.

7 Stir in the redcurrant jelly and add more salt and pepper if necessary. Serve hot.

Cook's tip

Red cabbage is a traditional accompaniment for game and meat dishes. It is also truly delicious served with sausages for a simple supper.

Turnips are in my opinion the most underrated of root vegetables. They are still often thought of as animal fodder, which is such a shame, and in Britain we have sadly become used to boiling turnips, which doesn't help their flavour. The best way to eat them is to choose early summer varieties and pick them when they are very small – the size of a clementine. Turnips can be roasted like potatoes or parboiled and finished with a glaze, as here. Use larger turnips only for purées or sliced in vegetable gratins.

GLAZED TURNIPS

Serves 4–6

900 g/2 lb young turnips, peeled and quartered

55 g/2 oz butter

1 tbsp brown sugar

150 ml/¼ pint vegetable stock

1 sprig of fresh rosemary

salt and pepper

1 Put the turnip into a saucepan of boiling salted water, bring back to the boil and simmer for 10 minutes. Drain well.

2 Melt the butter in the rinsed-out saucepan over a gentle heat, add the turnip and sugar and mix to coat well.

3 Add the stock with the rosemary and bring to the boil. Reduce the heat and simmer for 15–20 minutes with the lid off the pan so that the juices reduce and the turnips are tender and well glazed.

4 Remove the pan from the heat, discard the rosemary and season with salt and pepper to taste.

5 Serve immediately with roast lamb, pork, or duck.

VARIATION

Cook as above, but add honey instead of the sugar and add the juice of an orange to the stock. Serve garnished with a mixture of chopped parsley and grated orange rind.

Cauliflower cheese is nutritious, suitable for vegetarians and quite inexpensive. The type and amount of cheese is up to you. For a more substantial dish, add fried onions and bacon before the cheese sauce. A mixture of broccoli and cauliflower can be used to give a variation of flavours and textures. Sometimes wholemeal breadcrumbs are added to the Parmesan cheese to give a crunchier topping. This dish is often called by its French name cauliflower 'au gratin', which means cauliflower grilled or browned under a grill.

CAULIFLOWER CHEESE

Serves 4

1 cauliflower, trimmed and cut into florets (675 g/1½ lb prepared weight)

40 g/1½ oz butter

40 g/1½ oz plain flour

450 ml/16 fl oz milk

115 g/4 oz Cheddar cheese, finely grated

whole nutmeg, for grating

salt and pepper

1 tbsp grated Parmesan cheese

to serve

1 small tomato

green salad

crusty bread

1 Cook the cauliflower in a saucepan of boiling salted water for 4–5 minutes. It should still be firm. Drain, place in a hot 1.4-litre/2½-pint gratin dish and keep warm.

2 Melt the butter in the rinsed-out saucepan over a medium heat and stir in the flour. Cook for 1 minute, stirring continuously.

3 Remove from the heat and stir in the milk gradually until you have a smooth consistency.

4 Return to a low heat and continue to stir while the sauce comes to the boil and thickens. Reduce the heat and simmer gently, stirring constantly, for about 3 minutes until the sauce is creamy and smooth.

5 Remove from the heat and stir in the Cheddar cheese and a good grating of the nutmeg. Taste and season well with salt and pepper.

6 Pour the hot sauce over the cauliflower, top with the Parmesan and place under a hot grill to brown. Serve immediately with perhaps a tomato, green salad and some crusty bread.

Finding mushrooms growing wild is a real joy. If you've got a good eye and you know which varieties are edible, you can go out for a walk in the morning and come home with your breakfast, lunch or dinner. Sadly, these days it is not often you come across enough mushrooms to take home to cook. Luckily we can now find many varieties of mushrooms in the supermarkets that are cultivated, available throughout the year and can be used in a variety of dishes.

WAYS WITH MUSHROOMS

MUSHROOM RISOTTO

Fry 55 g/2 oz chopped streaky bacon in a large frying pan with 1 finely chopped onion, 25 g/1 oz butter and 1 tablespoon olive oil until the onion is a pale golden colour and the bacon has started to brown. Add 350 g/12 oz risotto rice and stir well. Have ready 1 litre/1¾ pints hot vegetable stock and slowly add a ladleful to the rice. Allow the rice to absorb the stock before adding the next ladleful, stirring constantly. Continue slowly adding stock until it is all used up: this will take 15–20 minutes. Stir in 175 g/6 oz sliced mushrooms (it is nice to use more exotic ones in this recipe if you can find them, like ceps, morels or shiitake. Otherwise use chestnut or field mushrooms). Allow to cook until the mushrooms have reduced and softened and the rice is just soft. Add a further 25 g/1 oz butter to the pan and season with salt and pepper to taste. Serve in warm bowls garnished with freshly chopped parsley. Serves 3–4.

MUSHROOMS IN GARLIC BUTTER

Melt 25 g/1 oz butter in a frying pan and add 2 tablespoons olive oil. Add 2 finely chopped garlic cloves and cook slowly until soft. Throw in 400 g/14 oz sliced chestnut mushrooms and stir around the pan until they absorb the oil and are softened. Add 2 tablespoons chopped fresh parsley and continue to cook for 1–2 minutes. Season well with salt and pepper and serve in warm bowls with lots of crusty bread to mop up the juices. Serves 2.

BAKED MUSHROOMS

Preheat the oven to 200°C/400°F/Gas Mark 6. Wipe 4 large flat mushrooms and cut out their stalks. Place the mushrooms in a baking dish and sprinkle over 2 finely chopped garlic cloves and 1 tablespoon finely chopped fresh thyme. Spoon in 4 tablespoons melted butter and squeeze in the juice of 1 lemon. Drizzle over 2 tablespoons olive oil and bake in the oven for 20–25 minutes, basting from time to time. These can be served with couscous or rice to make a good vegetarian supper dish, or with grilled meats or simply on toast. Serves 2.

MUSHROOMS IN RED WINE

Heat 25 g/1 oz butter in a frying pan, add 4 finely chopped shallots and 2 finely chopped garlic cloves. Cook for 1–2 minutes until the shallots are soft. Add 100 g/3½ oz whole shiitake mushrooms and the same weight of whole small chestnut mushrooms to the pan and stir well. Pour in 175 ml/6 fl oz beef or vegetable stock and 175 ml/6 fl oz red wine with 1 tablespoon chopped fresh thyme and allow to simmer until the sauce has reduced by half and the mushrooms are soft. Serve immediately. This can be served as a starter or as an accompaniment to steak. Serves 3–4.

We have a great tradition of growing vegetables and the variety that can be grown in the British Isles is huge, providing food for our table throughout the year. In spite of year-round availability in the supermarkets, it is still good to follow the seasons because this means we get the best of the crop at the right time, for the best price and at the peak of freshness. I have concentrated here on those vegetables that have traditionally been accompaniments to meat and fish dishes.

VEGETABLE ACCOMPANIMENTS

CARROT AND PARSNIP MASH

Cut 450 g/1 lb peeled parsnips and 450 g/1 lb peeled carrots into 5-cm/2-inch pieces and cook in boiling salted water for 10–15 minutes. Drain well and return to the pan. Mash using a potato masher and season well with salt and pepper. Add 55 g/2 oz butter and beat until smooth. Serve at once with a good grating of nutmeg on top. This is a wonderful accompaniment to any roast meat. Serves 4.

CABBAGE WEDGES

Cut a small white cabbage (about 550 g/1 lb 4 oz) into quarters and cook in a large saucepan of boiling salted water for 8–10 minutes. Drain well, season with salt, pepper and nutmeg and serve with a meat casserole. Serves 4.

STIR-FRIED CABBAGE

Finely shred 1 small white cabbage and fry in 2 tablespoons olive oil in a large frying pan over a high heat. Add 2 chopped garlic cloves and continue to fry until the cabbage is just tender. Season well with salt and pepper and add a little chopped stem ginger before serving – perhaps with chicken or sausages. Serves 4.

BRUSSELS SPROUTS

Try Brussels sprouts on other days apart from Christmas. Melt 25 g/1 oz butter in a saucepan and gently fry 1 chopped garlic clove and 2 tsp grated fresh root ginger for 1–2 minutes without browning. Add 500 g/1 lb 2 oz prepared sprouts and toss in the flavoured butter with 2 tablespoons water and the grated rind and juice of 1 orange, stirring well. Cover and cook over a medium heat for 3–4 minutes until the sprouts are just softening. Drain the sprouts and return the liquor to the pan. Bubble the sauce until really thick and pour over the sprouts before serving. Lovely with any roast meat. Serves 4.

GLAZED CARROTS AND LEEKS

Melt 25 g/1 oz butter in a saucepan and add 350 g/12 oz carrots cut at an angle into 1 cm/½ inch slices. Mix well to coat the carrots with the butter and add 150 ml/5 fl oz water. Cook gently over a medium heat for 3–4 minutes. Prepare the same weight of leeks in the same way and add to the pan. Mix in with the carrots and continue to cook for a further 2 minutes. Drain, add a further 25 g/1 oz butter and season well with salt and pepper before serving. Serves 4.

Today new varieties of 'designer' salad leaves can be found everywhere and it means we no longer have to have a plain salad of lettuce, tomato and cucumber on our plates. Herbs have always been grown in Britain, but now there is a renewed interest in using them and we are able to buy many more varieties than before, which means we can add interesting twists and flavours to our salads and other dishes. Particularly useful are the herbs sold in pots, which give us a fresh supply for days at a time.

GARDEN SALADS & HERBS

SIMPLE GARDEN SALAD

Take a handful of rocket and trim away any particularly long stems. Pick over a handful of lamb's lettuce and mizuna and tear some leaves of frisée into small pieces. Wash if necessary and make sure they are thoroughly dry. Place the salad leaves in a bowl and add a mixture of herbs, such as parsley, chervil and a few leaves of lemon thyme. Sprinkle over 2–3 tablespoons olive oil and 1 teaspoon freshly squeezed lemon juice and toss to coat the leaves. Add some sea salt crystals and a little pepper, toss again and serve. Serves 4.

TOMATO SALAD

A mixture of tomato varieties in a salad is good as it looks colourful and adds different flavours. Slice 2 beefsteak tomatoes horizontally and cut 4 plum tomatoes into quarters. Cut 12 red cherry tomatoes in half and the same number of gold cherry tomatoes (about 600 g/1 lb 5 oz tomatoes in total). Arrange the tomatoes in a shallow dish and sprinkle with ½ teaspoon sea salt and ½ teaspoon caster sugar and pour over 5 tablespoons olive oil. Scatter with a good handful of shredded basil and leave to stand for 30 minutes before serving to allow the flavours to mingle. Serves 4.

SPECIAL POTATO SALAD

The first waxy salad potatoes of the season are ideal for making a potato salad. Scrub 800 g/1 lb 12 oz small potatoes (Jersey Royals are my favourite) and cook in boiling salted water for 15–20 minutes until tender. Drain and halve the potatoes while still warm. Place in a serving dish and add 3 tablespoons chopped fresh mixed herbs (parsley, chives, basil and chervil). Pour over 6 tablespoons olive oil and 2 tablespoons white wine, season well with salt and pepper and toss the contents of the dish together. Serve while still warm. If you prefer, you could use a dressing of sour cream or crème fraîche. Serves 4.

GOOD COLESLAW

Shred half a hard white cabbage finely. Grate 2 carrots and core and slice 2 green apples. Chop 2 celery sticks and 3 spring onions finely. Place all the ingredients in a large bowl. In a small bowl, mix together 150 ml/5 fl oz mayonnaise and the same quantity of natural yogurt, add 1 teaspoon French mustard and 1 tablespoon lemon juice and season well with salt and pepper. Pour the dressing over the salad vegetables and mix well. If liked, you could add 40 g/1½ oz raisins and the same amount of chopped walnuts. Serve the coleslaw garnished with a sprinkling of chopped fresh mixed herbs. Serves 4.

6

PUDDINGS & DESSERTS

Most people enjoy puddings and desserts although in these more health-conscious times we know that too many of them add a disproportionate amount of sugar and animal fat to our diet. The majority of us now lead sedentary lives and don't take enough exercise to eat puddings daily, and so fresh fruit or low-fat yogurt are a more usual end of a meal. But at weekends or on special occasions a treat is reasonable, particularly if it is one of our famed hot puddings for wintry days. We have always been a nation of pudding eaters, probably because our wet and wintry climate means we need hot, filling puddings to warm us through and satisfy our appetites. These puddings have a great worldwide reputation, particularly in France where the rest of our cooking is not greatly respected, and the British are certainly the masters of the art of pudding making. The name 'pudding' is the term given to those sweets that are prepared by steaming or baking and served hot. Cold or uncooked dishes are usually called 'desserts'.

The British have always made fruit puddings because historically we have produced a lot of fruit in these isles. The traditional fruits are apples, pears, plums, rhubarb, gooseberries and blackberries. Often in autumn there is a glut of fruit so making the surplus into puddings is an ideal way of using it.

Steamed suet puddings were very popular in the past because they were filling and cheap to make. They could be flavoured with any fruit that might be available and sweetened with honey or sugar. Happily, these old favourites are now becoming popular again and are seen on restaurant menus, prompting us to cook them again at home, too. It's pleasing to see their renewed popularity – but you might want to plan a hearty walk before you enjoy them!

Milk puddings have been eaten since medieval times and are comfort food at its best. Creamy milk mixed with rice and cooked slowly in a low oven with a little sugar makes a wonderful pudding for all ages. Extra jam or fruit can be served with rice pudding to ring the changes. The more creamy desserts were devised to use our excellent dairy produce and give very rich sweets like syllabubs and fruit fools.

Bread-based puddings, the best of which is bread and butter pudding, have always been popular. Bread was considered to be more easily digestible than the more fatty pastry used to make tarts and pies, so these lighter puddings were introduced for the young and the elderly. Others that make use of bread include summer pudding and queen of puddings.

Pies and pastry puddings are of course popular perennials, the most famous of which is our homely apple pie. Everyone has a favourite recipe for apple pie, some use cooking apples, some eating apples and some half and half. The type of pastry, whether there should be a top and bottom of pastry or not, and whether other ingredients should be added are all individual choices, but each family seems to have its special way. A more modest version of a hot fruit pudding is a crumble, in which any fruit can be used and then the rubbed-in crumble is simply sprinkled on the top before baking.

Special-occasion puddings would include trifle, lemon meringue pie and upside-down pudding. These are often served for celebrations or Sunday lunches with the family, but they are just as popular for dinner parties where indulgent puddings always make a welcome treat. Cold desserts that contain fruit and cream are often set with gelatine to produce mousses and soufflés. Ice creams and sorbets are now easily made using domestic ice-cream makers.

Today, as most of us have to watch our waistlines, puddings have been relegated to special occasions and not everyday eating. As a substitute we eat fresh fruit and yogurt, which is healthier and (almost) equally delicious.

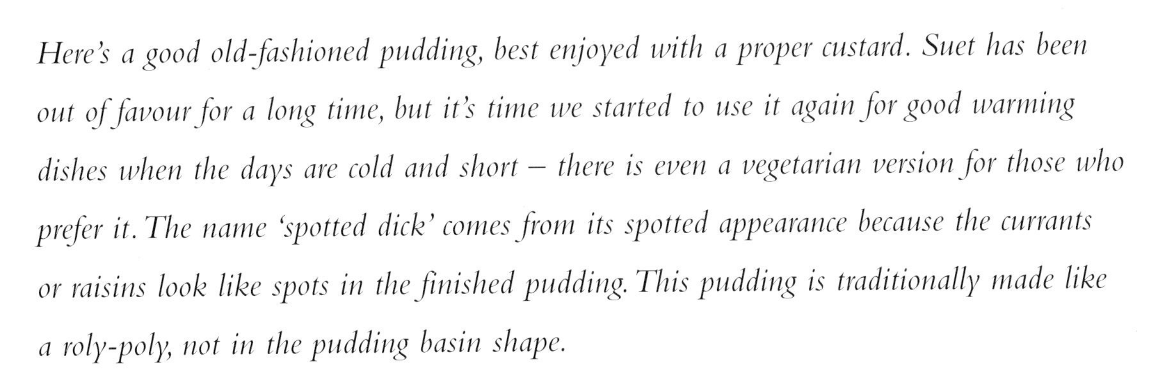

Here's a good old-fashioned pudding, best enjoyed with a proper custard. Suet has been out of favour for a long time, but it's time we started to use it again for good warming dishes when the days are cold and short – there is even a vegetarian version for those who prefer it. The name 'spotted dick' comes from its spotted appearance because the currants or raisins look like spots in the finished pudding. This pudding is traditionally made like a roly-poly, not in the pudding basin shape.

SPOTTED DICK & CUSTARD

Serves 6

225 g/8 oz self-raising flour

115 g/4 oz suet

55 g/2 oz caster sugar

140 g/5 oz currants or raisins

grated rind of 1 lemon

150–175 ml/5–6 fl oz milk

2 tsp melted butter, for greasing

for the custard

425 ml/15 fl oz single cream

5 egg yolks

3 tbsp caster sugar

½ tsp vanilla extract

1 tsp cornflour (optional)

1 Mix together the flour, suet, sugar, currants and lemon rind in a mixing bowl.

2 Pour in the milk and stir together to give a fairly soft dough.

3 Turn out onto a floured surface and roll into a cylinder. Wrap in greaseproof paper that has been well-buttered and seal the ends, allowing room for the pudding to rise. Over wrap with foil and place in a steamer over a saucepan of boiling water.

4 Steam for about 1–1½ hours, checking the water level in the saucepan from time to time.

5 To make the custard, heat the cream in a small saucepan just to boiling point. Cream the egg yolks, sugar and vanilla extract together in a measuring jug. You can add the cornflour to this cold egg yolk mixture to ensure the sauce does not separate. Pour the hot cream into the jug, stirring all the time. Return the mixture to the saucepan.

6 Heat the custard very gently, stirring constantly, until the sauce has just thickened, then remove from the heat. Alternatively, you can cook the custard in a bowl over a saucepan of simmering water to prevent overcooking.

7 Remove the pudding from the steamer and unwrap. Place on a hot plate and cut into thick slices. Serve with lots of custard.

Is this the nation's favourite pudding? A hot pudding steamed to give a light, moist sponge just oozing with syrup. Children and adults alike love it. This recipe can also be followed to make a fruit sponge pudding using a layer of stewed fruit in the basin instead of the syrup. A jam, marmalade or mincemeat pudding can be made in the same way. To make a chocolate pudding, replace 25 g/1 oz flour with cocoa powder and serve with a chocolate sauce – my favourite.

STEAMED SYRUP SPONGE PUDDING

Serves 6

butter, for greasing

2 tbsp golden syrup, plus extra to serve

115 g/4 oz butter

115 g/4 oz caster sugar

2 eggs, lightly beaten

175 g/6 oz self-raising flour

2 tbsp milk

grated rind of 1 lemon

1 Butter a 1.2-litre/2-pint pudding basin and put the syrup into the bottom.

2 Beat together the butter and sugar until soft and creamy, then beat in the eggs, a little at a time.

3 Fold in the flour and stir in the milk to make a soft dropping consistency. Add the lemon rind. Turn the mixture into the pudding basin.

4 Cover the surface with a circle of greaseproof or baking paper and top with a pleated sheet of foil. Secure with some string or crimp the edges of the foil to ensure a tight fit around the basin.

5 Place the pudding in a large saucepan half-filled with boiling water. Cover the saucepan and bring back to the boil over a medium heat. Reduce the heat to a slow simmer and steam for 1½ hours until risen and firm. Keep checking the water level and top up with boiling water as necessary.

6 Remove the pan from the heat and lift out the pudding basin. Remove the cover and loosen the pudding from the sides of the basin using a knife.

7 Turn out into a warmed dish and heat a little more syrup to serve with the pudding.

Sometimes known as an 'upside-down cake', this is a creamed cake mixture that is baked with fruit under it so that when it is turned out, the fruit is on top and looks decorative. It has a lovely rich butter and sugar topping as well, which gives the pudding an attractive and glossy appearance. A good custard sauce or some thick cream would be good with this pudding.

UPSIDE-DOWN PUDDING

Serves 6–8

225 g/8 oz unsalted butter

55 g/2 oz soft brown sugar

14–16 hazelnuts

600 g/1 lb 5 oz canned apricot halves, drained

175 g/6 oz demerara sugar

3 eggs, beaten

175 g/6 oz self-raising flour

55 g/2 oz ground hazelnuts

2 tablespoons milk

cream or Custard (see page 177), to serve

1 Preheat the oven to 180°C/350°F/Gas Mark 4.

2 Grease a 25-cm/10-inch cake tin and line the base with baking paper.

3 Cream 55 g/2 oz of the butter with the soft brown sugar and spread over the base of the tin.

4 Place a hazelnut in each apricot half and invert onto the base. The apricots should cover the whole surface.

5 Cream the demerara sugar together with the remaining butter until pale and fluffy, then beat in the eggs gradually. Fold in the flour and the ground hazelnuts together with the milk and spread the mixture over the apricots.

6 Bake in the centre of the oven for about 45 minutes until the pudding is golden brown and well risen. Run a knife around the edge of the pudding and invert onto a warm serving plate. Serve warm with cream or Custard.

VARIATIONS

You could use slices of pineapple and glacé cherries as the topping, and ground almonds instead of hazelnuts in the sponge. Alternatively, use pear halves with walnuts or canned cherries and add 2 tablespoons cocoa instead of the nuts to make a chocolate sponge. To make a ginger sponge, add 1 tablespoon ground ginger to the mixture and use rhubarb. Add the grated zest of l lemon to the sponge mixture to make a lemon sponge and pair with strawberries or raspberries.

A classic British pudding made with suet pastry. This is true rib-sticking stuff – lots of hot gooey pastry and strawberry jam. It needs steaming in a steamer because it is made in the traditional roll shape, not in a basin. A favourite pudding in proper school dinners, a jam roly-poly is always welcome, but particularly on a cold winter's day. A good custard sauce must be served with this pudding. Cream will not do, although a serving of jam sauce goes down well.

JAM ROLY-POLY

Serves 6

225 g/8 oz self-raising flour

pinch of salt

115 g/4 oz suet

grated rind of 1 lemon

1 tbsp sugar

125 ml/4 fl oz mixed milk and water

4-6 tbsp strawberry jam

2 tablespoons milk

Custard (see page 177), to serve

1 Sift the flour into a mixing bowl and add the salt and suet. Mix together well. Stir in the lemon rind and the sugar.

2 Make a well in the centre and add the liquid to give a light, elastic dough. Knead lightly until smooth. If you have time, wrap the dough in clingfilm and leave it to rest for 30 minutes.

3 Roll the dough into a 20 x 25-cm/8 x 10-inch rectangle.

4 Spread the jam over the dough, leaving a 1 cm/½ inch border. Brush the border with the milk and roll up the dough carefully, like a Swiss roll, from one short end. Seal the ends.

5 Wrap the roly-poly loosely in greaseproof paper and then in foil, sealing the ends well.

6 Prepare a steamer by half filling it with water and putting it on to boil. Place the roly-poly in the steamer and steam over rapidly boiling water for 1½–2 hours, making sure you top up the water from time to time.

7 When cooked, remove from the steamer, unwrap and serve on a warm plate, cut into slices with warm custard.

VARIATIONS

Use the same amount of mincemeat instead of jam to make a mincemeat roly-poly. Alternatively, use golden syrup instead of the jam and serve with extra hot syrup. Lemon curd or marmalade can also be used.

Rice pudding is definitely nursery food, some people love it, some loathe it, but it is still a very soothing food whether you are old, young or just under the weather. Milk puddings have been popular for centuries and were thought to be good for you. Certainly milk is nourishing, and mixed with starch and sugar makes a pleasant dish. Other grains like tapioca and semolina can also be used, but are not as popular as rice. The topic of 'skin' is a controversial issue – some discard it, while others fight over it!

BAKED RICE PUDDING

Serves 4–6

1 tbsp melted butter

115 g/4 oz pudding rice

55 g/2 oz caster sugar

850 ml/1½ pints full-cream milk

½ tsp vanilla extract

40 g/1½ oz unsalted butter

whole nutmeg, for grating

cream, jam, fruit, honey or ice cream, to serve

1 Preheat the oven to 300°C/150°F/Gas Mark 2. Grease a 1.2-litre/2-pint baking dish (a gratin dish is good) with the melted butter, place the rice in the dish and sprinkle with the sugar.

2 Heat the milk in a saucepan until almost boiling, then pour over the rice. Add the vanilla extract and stir well to dissolve the sugar.

3 Cut the butter into small pieces and scatter over the surface of the pudding.

4 Grate the whole nutmeg over the top, using as much as you like to give a good covering.

5 Place the dish on a baking tray and bake in the centre of the oven for 1½–2 hours until the pudding is well browned on the top. You can stir it after the first half hour to disperse the rice.

6 Serve hot with some cream, jam, fresh fruit puree, stewed fruit or ice cream. It is also good cold with fresh fruit, honey or ice cream.

VARIATIONS

To make a richer pudding, use half cream and half milk. Other flavours can be used instead of the nutmeg – try grated lemon zest, orange flower water, rosewater, cardamom, cinnamon or mixed spice. Even chocolate can be added, either some chocolate powder added with the milk or roughly chopped pieces sprinkled in towards the end of the cooking time. A tot of rum, brandy or whisky is also good.

This was a very popular pudding on feast days and holidays. It looks very exotic, yet is simply made from breadcrumbs, eggs and milk, then topped with jam and meringue, which make it delicious and indulgent! You can make it using fruit instead of jam – a layer of apple purée or fresh raspberries is good – and a few flaked almonds scattered over the meringue before cooking give a lovely crunchy addition. I like to serve these puddings in individual dishes for dinner parties.

QUEEN OF PUDDINGS

Serves 4–6

2 tbsp butter

600 ml/1 pint milk

115 g/4 oz fresh white breadcrumbs

115 g/4 oz caster sugar

grated rind of 1 lemon

3 eggs, separated

3 tbsp raspberry jam, warmed

1 tsp golden granulated sugar

1 Preheat the oven to 180°C/350°F/Gas Mark 4.

2 Using a little of the butter, grease a 1-litre/1¾-pint baking dish.

3 Heat the remaining butter in the saucepan with the milk and gently bring to the boil over a medium heat.

4 Remove from the heat and stir in the breadcrumbs, 1 tablespoon of the caster sugar and the lemon rind.

5 Allow to stand and cool for 15 minutes, then beat in the egg yolks.

6 Pour the mixture into the baking dish, smooth the surface and bake in the centre of the oven for about 30 minutes until it is set. Spread over the jam.

7 Whisk the egg whites in the mixing bowl until very thick, then gradually add the remaining caster sugar. Continue until all the sugar has been added.

8 Spoon the meringue over the pudding and make sure the meringue covers it completely. Swirl the meringue into attractive peaks and sprinkle with the granulated sugar.

9 Bake again in the centre of the oven for 10–15 minutes until the meringue is golden brown but still soft. Serve warm.

BAKERY

Bakewell pudding, or tart as it is often known, hails from the town of Bakewell in Derbyshire. There seem to have been two sorts of Bakewell pudding. One was a puff pastry case with a layer of jam and a rich custard topping. The other was a shortcrust pastry base, also with jam, but covered with an almond-flavoured sponge mixture. The latter is the one more generally known and certainly the one commercially produced. This recipe is close to the original pudding, but includes a small amount of almonds.

BAKEWELL PUDDING

Serves 4–6

225 g/8 oz ready-made puff pastry

4 tbsp strawberry jam

4 egg yolks

1 egg white

175 g/6 oz caster sugar

115 g/4 oz butter

25 g/1 oz ground almonds

cream or Custard (see page 177), to serve

1 Preheat the oven to 200°C/400°F/Gas Mark 6.

2 Roll out the puff pastry and use to line a 23-cm/9-inch tart tin.

3 Spread the jam over the base to give a good layer.

4 Beat the egg yolks and egg white together in a bowl and beat in the sugar.

5 Melt the butter in a small saucepan over a medium heat until it is almost colouring and pour it, while still bubbling, into the egg mixture, beating well.

6 Fold in the ground almonds and pour the mixture over the jam in the pastry case.

7 Bake in the oven on a preheated baking sheet for 15 minutes, then reduce the temperature to 180°C/ 350°F/Gas Mark 4 and continue to cook for a further 30 minutes until the pudding is lightly browned and the pastry crisp.

8 The pudding is best served straight from the oven with single cream or a thin custard.

Wensleydale is one of the Yorkshire Dales which produces superb dairy products and is particularly famous for its fine cheese. A smooth, mild cheese with a pleasant sharpness, Wensleydale used to be made from sheep's milk, but now it is made from cow's milk. It is said that a Yorkshireman always eats cheese with apple pie and, I believe, with mince pies too. This recipe uses the cheese in the pastry and also serves a little extra with the hot pie so that it melts while being eaten. You won't need any cream.

WENSLEYDALE APPLE PIE

Serves 6–8

butter, for greasing

350 g/12 oz plain flour

pinch of salt

100 g/3½ oz butter

100 g/3½ oz Wensleydale cheese, grated

2 egg yolks

3 tbsp cold water

900 g/2 lb cooking apples, peeled, cored and thinly sliced

115 g/4 oz caster sugar

½ tsp ground cinnamon

½ tsp ground cloves

1 egg white

175 g/6 oz Wensleydale cheese, sliced, to serve

1 Grease a 23-cm/9-inch tart tin.

2 Sift the flour and salt into a mixing bowl and gently rub in the butter until the mixture resembles breadcrumbs. Add the grated cheese and rub in also. Add the egg yolks and mix together with the water to form a soft dough.

3 Knead lightly until the pastry is smooth. Cover with clingfilm and chill for 30 minutes.

4 Preheat the oven to 200°C/400°F/Gas Mark 6.

5 Roll out two-thirds of the pastry and use to line the tin.

6 Layer in the sliced apples with all but 1 teaspoon of the sugar and the spices.

7 Roll out the remaining pastry, dampen the edges of the pastry lining the tin and lay the rolled pastry on top. Press down well to seal the edges and cut away any excess pastry. Crimp the edges with a fork.

8 Beat the egg white and use to glaze the pie, sprinkling the remaining sugar over to give a crisp finish.

9 Bake in the oven for 40–45 minutes until the pastry is crisp and golden.

10 Cut the pie into portions and slip a slice of cheese under the crust of each piece before serving.

Crumble is one of the simplest puddings, easy to make and delicious to eat. Children enjoy learning how to rub in the butter with the flour. Any fruit can be used, but rhubarb is particularly British. The first, forced shoots are the sweetest and the most tender. Ginger is often added to improve the flavour, but I prefer a little orange to add to the taste. The crumble topping can be made with white or brown flour, and some nuts may be added if liked.

RHUBARB CRUMBLE

Serves 6

900 g/2 lb rhubarb

115 g/4 oz caster sugar

grated rind and juice of 1 orange

cream, yogurt or Custard (see page 177), to serve

for the crumble

225 g/8 oz plain or wholemeal flour

115 g/4 oz butter

115 g/4 oz soft brown sugar

1 tsp ground ginger

1 Preheat the oven to 190°C/375°F/Gas Mark 5.

2 Cut the rhubarb into 2.5-cm/1-inch lengths and place in a 1.7-litre/3-pint ovenproof dish with the sugar and the orange rind and juice.

3 Make the crumble by placing the flour in a mixing bowl and rubbing in the butter until the mixture resembles breadcrumbs. Stir in the sugar and the ginger.

4 Spread the crumble evenly over the fruit and press down lightly using a fork.

5 Bake in the centre of the oven on a baking tray for 25–30 minutes until the crumble is golden brown.

6 Serve warm with cream, yogurt or custard.

Apple Charlotte is the name given to a pudding prepared for Queen Charlotte, wife of George III, by her French cooks. Apparently she was a patron of apple growers at the time, which is why the dish was so named. It consists of pieces of bread dipped in melted butter and used to line a 'Charlotte' mould. The bread mould was then filled with apple purée, covered with more buttered bread and baked to give a crisp brown crust on both the top and the bottom. This version uses blackberries as well as apples.

BLACKBERRY AND APPLE CHARLOTTE

Serves 6

100 g/3½ oz butter

175 g/6 oz caster sugar

450 g/1 lb cooking apples, peeled, cored and cut into 1-cm/½-inch pieces

450 g/1 lb blackberries

grated rind and juice of 1 lemon

6–8 slices of day-old white bread, crusts removed

cream, to serve

1 Melt the butter and brush the inside of a 15-cm/6-inch Charlotte mould or cake tin. Spoon 2 tablespoons of the sugar into the mould and move the mould around so that the sides are evenly coated with the sugar.

2 Place both the fruits in a saucepan with the lemon rind and juice and cook over a low heat until they are soft. Continue to cook for about 10–12 minutes until all the liquid has evaporated and you have a very thick pulp.

3 Preheat the oven to 200°C/400°F/Gas Mark 6.

4 Cut the bread into 2 rounds the size of the base and top of the mould. Cut the remaining bread into 4-cm/1½-inch fingers. Dip the smaller round into the remaining melted butter and place in the base of the mould. Use the bread fingers to line the mould, brushing or dipping all the pieces in the butter. Make sure the bread is arranged closely round the edges of the mould.

5 Add all but 1 teaspoon of the remaining sugar to the fruit pulp, stir well and check the sweetness. Add a little more sugar if required.

6 Fill the bread mould with the fruit mixture and press down well. Cover with the remaining round of bread, which should also be buttered. Sprinkle over the remaining teaspoon of sugar.

7 Cook in the centre of the oven for 40–45 minutes until the top is golden brown and crispy.

8 Loosen the pudding using a round-bladed knife and turn out onto a deep serving plate. Serve hot with some cream.

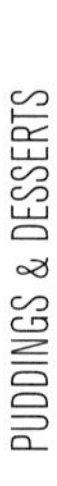

For years bread and butter pudding was poorly regarded because it was often made with dry leftover bread. The resurgence in popularity of the pudding is due to clever cooks using good-quality ingredients and adding fresh eggs and some cream to enrich the pudding, so that it has now become fashionable again in restaurants up and down the country. It can be made with plain bread, malt bread or with slices of fruit, and the fruit can be varied according to taste.

BREAD & BUTTER PUDDING

Serves 4–6

85 g/3 oz butter, softened

6 slices of thick white bread

55 g/2 oz mixed fruit (sultanas, currants and raisins)

25 g/1 oz candied peel

3 large eggs

300 ml/½ pint milk

150 ml/¼ pint double cream

55 g/2 oz caster sugar

whole nutmeg, for grating

1 tbsp demerara sugar

cream, to serve

1 Preheat the oven to 180°C/350°F/Gas Mark 4.

2 Use a little of the butter to grease a 20 x 25-cm/8 x 10-inch baking dish and butter the slices of bread. Cut the bread into quarters and arrange half overlapping in the dish.

3 Scatter half the fruit and peel over the bread, cover with the remaining bread slices and add the remaining fruit and peel.

4 In a mixing jug, whisk the eggs well and mix in the milk, cream and sugar. Pour this over the pudding and leave to stand for 15 minutes to allow the bread to soak up some of the egg mixture. Tuck in most of the fruit as you don't want it to burn in the oven. Grate the nutmeg over the top of the pudding, according to taste, and sprinkle over the demerara sugar.

5 Place the pudding on a baking tray and bake at the top of the oven for 30–40 minutes until just set and golden brown.

6 Remove from the oven and serve warm with a little pouring cream.

VARIATIONS

You can use dried apricots instead of the mixed fruit and spread a little apricot jam on the buttered bread. Alternatively, add a sliced banana to the pudding and sprinkle with a little cinnamon or add sliced pears and use slices of panettone, adding some vanilla extract to the egg mixture. For a grown-up pudding, pour a small glass of rum or whisky into the egg mixture.

This Scottish dessert seems to have evolved over time. It started as a 'crowdie', which was a simple oatmeal gruel, then progressed to becoming a 'cream crowdie' when it was served with cream. It became 'cranachan' when the oatmeal was first toasted to give a better flavour and texture and honey or sugar was added. Whisky was also sometimes mixed in to give it a real Scottish flavour. Raspberries are a sharp contrast to the cream.

RASPBERRY CRANACHAN

Serves 6

85 g/3 oz medium oatmeal

425 ml/¾ pint whipping cream

2 tbsp clear honey

2 tbsp whisky

400 g/14 oz fresh raspberries

1 Toast the oatmeal lightly, either in a frying pan over a low heat or under a hot grill. It should be golden brown but not too dark or the dessert will be bitter. Leave to cool.

2 Lightly whip the cream with the honey and whisky using an electric mixer until the mixture forms soft peaks. Fold in most of the toasted oatmeal, reserving a tablespoon for decoration.

3 Spoon half of the raspberries into 6 individual glass dishes and spoon in half the cream and oatmeal mixture. Top with the remaining raspberries and the remaining cream mixture, smoothing over the surfaces.

4 Serve soon after mixing while the oats are still crunchy. Scatter the reserved oats on top of the glasses to decorate.

VARIATION

Some recipes use marmalade and orange segments to flavour the dessert, which is again a Scottish undertone as marmalade is a traditional product of Scotland.

In the Middle Ages, the cream and wine confection now called a syllabub was sometimes called a 'flummery' or 'posset'. It is alleged that originally the cow was milked directly into a jug of wine to make a froth or foam. Through time, the foam has become more important than the drink and a thicker dessert has evolved. Wine or sherry can be used depending on the sweetness required, and the amount of lemon adjusted according to taste. Some syllabubs separate after several hours; this one keeps its solid state for a day.

SYLLABUB

Serves 4–6

grated rind and juice of 1 lemon

125 ml/4 fl oz sweet white wine

2 tbsp brandy

55 g/2 oz caster sugar

300 ml/½ pint double cream

zest of 1 lemon, to decorate

sponge fingers or ratafia biscuits, to serve

1 Place the rind and the juice of the lemon in a bowl together with the wine and brandy. Cover and leave to infuse for a few hours or overnight.

2 Stir in the sugar until it has dissolved.

3 Whip the cream in a large bowl using an electric mixer. When it starts to thicken, carefully pour in the liquid, a little at a time, until it is all mixed in. The mixture should be very thick and soft, do not overwhip it.

4 Spoon into small glasses and chill for a few hours. This can be made a day ahead.

5 Decorate with the lemon zest sprinkled on top. Sponge fingers or ratafia biscuits can be served with the dessert.

VARIATIONS

Syllabub can be made with cassis or crème de framboise to give a pretty pink colour. It can also be layered with fruit such as raspberries.

Even in today's sophisticated times, young children love jelly. A colourful array of jellies, topped with cream and hundreds and thousands or served with ice cream, is the highlight of a birthday tea. Jelly is made from a variety of fruit juices and set using gelatine. Gelatine can be bought in powdered form or as gelatine leaves, but the powders are the easier to use. The two recipes below are for 'grown-up' jellies, which can be served for a dinner-party dessert.

JELLY

ORANGE JELLY

Serves 4

grated rind of 2 oranges

550 ml/19 fl oz freshly squeezed orange juice

115 g/4 oz caster sugar

50 ml/2 fl oz Cointreau (optional)

11 g/¼ oz sachet of powdered gelatine

3 tbsp water

8 strawberries, sliced

1 Put the orange rind and 150 ml/5 fl oz of the juice into a saucepan. Add the sugar and heat until dissolved. Remove from the heat and steep for 15 minutes. Strain through a muslin-lined sieve. Add the remaining juice and the Cointreau, if using. You should have 600 ml/1 pint liquid.

2 In a cup, dissolve the gelatine in the water and leave for 1–2 minutes until it is spongy. Place the cup in a small saucepan with enough water to come halfway up the sides and heat gently for 2–3 minutes to dissolve the gelatine, which should be clear. Cool until it is the same temperature as the fruit juice then add it to the juice and stir well.

3 Put the strawberries in 4 small dishes. Pour in the jelly and chill until set.

BLACKCURRANT JELLY

Serves 4–6

450 g/1 lb blackcurrants

150 ml/¼ pint water

225 g/8 oz caster sugar

175 ml/6 fl oz port

11 g/¼ oz sachet of powdered gelatine

3 tbsp water

cream, to serve

1 Put the blackcurrants, water and sugar into a saucepan and cook slowly over a medium heat until they are soft. Remove from the heat and pour the contents of the pan into a sieve. Push the fruit through the sieve until you have a smooth purée. Pour the purée into a measuring jug and add the port. Make up to 600 ml/1 pint liquid with extra water.

2 Dissolve the gelatine as in step 2 above. Cool until it is the same temperature as the fruit mixture then mix the two together and pour into a glass serving bowl. Chill until set.

Trifle always includes cake soaked in sherry, some fruit, custard and cream. A proper custard is called for, but if time is short, you can cheat by using one of the freshly prepared chilled custards available now, which are really good. Any fruit can be used, fresh or canned, and the topping should be whipped cream. The traditional decoration is hundreds and thousands but if you have used really good ingredients I would suggest some whole toasted almonds or silver dragées.

TRIFLE

Serves 6–8

8 trifle sponges or 1 layer of Victoria sandwich cake (see page 236)

115 g/4 oz raspberry jam

150 ml/¼ pint sherry

55 g/2 oz small macaroons or ratafia biscuits

2 tbsp brandy

350 g/12 oz raspberries, fresh or frozen

568 ml/1 pint Custard (see page 177 or bought), cooled

300 ml/½ pint double cream

2 tbsp milk

40 g/1½ oz toasted flaked almonds or silver dragées, to decorate

1 Break the sponges or cake into pieces and spread with the jam.

2 Place in a large glass serving bowl and pour over the sherry.

3 Add the macaroons to the bowl and sprinkle over the brandy.

4 Spoon the raspberries on top.

5 Pour over the Custard, cover the bowl with clingfilm and leave to settle for 2–3 hours or overnight.

6 Just before serving, whip the cream with the milk until it is thick but still soft. Spoon over the custard and swirl around using a knife to give an attractive appearance. Decorate as desired with almonds or dragées and serve chilled.

VARIATIONS

You can use the Syllabub (see page 201) as a topping and omit the custard and cream. Alternatively, a 'Black Forest' trifle can be made using Morello cherry jam and chocolate cake. Black cherries (fresh or canned) may be used and the top of the trifle decorated with 2 tablespoons grated chocolate.

This is one of the few uncooked puddings. It is made in the traditional pudding shape with slices of bread and a variety of summer fruits – hence the name. This pudding was in fact devised in the nineteenth century as an invalid food when pastry was considered too rich for convalescents. You can vary the fruits according to what is available, but it is not a good idea to use strawberries because they are too soft for this pudding. In the autumn, a similar pudding can be made using stewed apples and blackberries.

SUMMER PUDDING

Serves 6

675 g/1 lb 8 oz mixed soft fruits, such as redcurrants, blackcurrants, raspberries and blackberries

140 g/5 oz caster sugar

2 tbsp crème de framboise liqueur (optional)

6–8 slices of good day-old white bread, crusts removed

double cream, to serve

1 You will need an 850-ml/1½-pint pudding basin.

2 Place the fruits in a large saucepan with the sugar.

3 Over a low heat, very slowly bring to the boil, stirring carefully to ensure that the sugar has dissolved. Cook over a low heat for only 2–3 minutes until the juices run but the fruit still holds its shape. Add the liqueur if using.

4 Line the pudding basin with some of the slices of bread (cut them to shape so that the bread fits well). Spoon in the cooked fruit and juices, reserving a little of the juice for later.

5 Cover the surface of the fruit with the remaining bread. Place a saucer on top of the pudding and weight it down for at least 8 hours or overnight in the refrigerator.

6 Turn out the pudding and pour over the reserved juices to colour any white bits of bread that may be showing. Serve with the thick cream.

This delectable dessert is from a very traditional British background: Eton College. On the 4th of June every year there is a celebration at the school and this dessert is always served. It is a sort of strawberry fool, which started out as a simple concoction of strawberries and cream flavoured with sugar and vanilla, mixed together to give a 'mess'. Today the recipe has developed into a richer, truly wonderful 'mess' of strawberries, cream and crushed meringue. Try other berries too, such as raspberries, redcurrants or a mixture.

ETON MESS

Serves 4–6

3 egg whites

175 g/6 oz caster sugar

700 g/1 lb 9 oz strawberries

2 tbsp icing sugar

2 tbsp crème de fraise (strawberry) liqueur (optional)

300 ml/½ pint double cream

150 ml/¼ pint single cream

1 Preheat the oven to 150°C/300°F/Gas Mark 2.

2 Whisk the egg whites in a mixing bowl using an electric mixer until thick and in soft peaks. Add the sugar gradually, whisking well with each addition. The meringue mixture should be glossy and firm.

3 Spoon the meringue onto a baking tray lined with baking paper and spread into a rough 30-cm/12-inch round. Cook for 45–50 minutes until the meringue is firm on the outside but still soft in the centre. Remove from the oven and allow to cool.

4 Check over the strawberries and hull them.

5 Place a third of the berries (choose the larger ones) in a liquidizer and purée with the icing sugar. Pour the purée into a bowl, add the liqueur, if using, and the remaining strawberries and turn in the sauce until well mixed.

6 Whip together the double and single cream until thick but still light and floppy.

7 Break the meringue into large pieces and place half in a large glass serving bowl. Spoon over half the fruit mixture and half the cream. Layer up the remaining ingredients and lightly fold the mixtures together so you have a streaky appearance.

8 Serve soon after mixing or the meringues will soften.

Gooseberries like to grow in cooler areas and do well in the north of England and Scotland. In the past, gooseberry sauce was served with oily fish such as mackerel or fatty meats like goose because the sharp taste was an ideal complement. These gooseberries used to be very sour, but new varieties have been developed that are sweeter and are becoming more popular for use in desserts. They were cooked with a couple of sprigs of elder blossom to enhance their flavour, but today we can use elderflower cordial.

GOOSEBERRY FOOL

Serves 6

700 g/1 lb 9 oz gooseberries

25 g/1 oz butter

115 g/4 oz caster sugar

1 tbsp elderflower cordial

300 ml/½ pint double cream

crisp biscuits, to serve

1 Top and tail the gooseberries and place in a saucepan with the butter.

2 Over a gentle heat slowly bring to the boil, stirring constantly, until the gooseberries are soft and turning yellow.

3 Remove from the heat and crush the berries with a wooden spoon until you have a thick purée.

4 Add the sugar and stir until dissolved, then add the elderflower cordial. You might like to taste for sweetness at this point and add a little more sugar if needed. Allow to cool.

5 Whip the cream until it is thick but not too dry. Using a metal spoon, fold in the cold gooseberry purée carefully. Only just combine the cream and the purée – the fool looks more attractive if it has a marbled effect.

6 Spoon into 6 glass serving dishes or 1 large glass bowl and chill well. Serve with crisp biscuits.

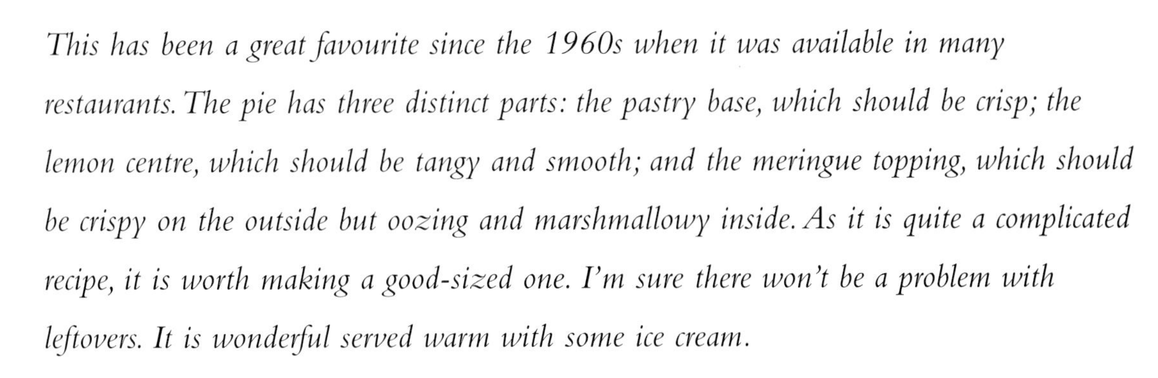

This has been a great favourite since the 1960s when it was available in many restaurants. The pie has three distinct parts: the pastry base, which should be crisp; the lemon centre, which should be tangy and smooth; and the meringue topping, which should be crispy on the outside but oozing and marshmallowy inside. As it is quite a complicated recipe, it is worth making a good-sized one. I'm sure there won't be a problem with leftovers. It is wonderful served warm with some ice cream.

LEMON MERINGUE PIE

Serves 8–10

butter, for greasing

plain flour, for dusting

250 g/9 oz ready-rolled pastry, thawed if frozen

3 tbsp cornflour

85 g/3 oz caster sugar

grated rind of 3 lemons

300 ml/½ pint cold water

150 ml/¼ pint lemon juice

3 egg yolks

55 g/2 oz unsalted butter, cut into small cubes

for the meringue

3 egg whites

175 g/6 oz caster sugar

1 tsp golden granulated sugar

1 Grease a 25-cm/10-inch fluted flan tin. On a lightly floured work surface, roll out the pastry into a circle 5 cm/2 inches larger than the flan tin. Ease the pastry into the tin without stretching and press down lightly into the corners. Roll off the excess pastry to neaten the pastry case. Prick the base of the flan base and chill, uncovered, in the refrigerator for 20–30 minutes.

2 Preheat the oven to 200°C/400°F/Gas Mark 6. Line the pastry case with baking paper and fill with baking beans. Bake on a heated baking tray for 15 minutes. Remove the beans and paper and return to the oven for 10 minutes until the pastry is dry and just colouring. Remove from the oven and reduce the temperature to 150°C/300°F/Gas Mark 2.

3 Put the cornflour, sugar and lemon rind into a saucepan. Pour in a little of the water and blend to a smooth paste. Gradually add the remaining water and the lemon juice. Place the saucepan over a medium heat and bring the mixture to the boil, stirring continuously. Simmer gently for 1 minute until smooth and glossy. Remove the saucepan from the heat and beat in the egg yolks, 1 at a time, then beat in the butter. Place the saucepan in a bowl of cold water to cool the filling. When cool, spoon the mixture into the pastry case.

4 To make the meringue, whisk the egg whites using an electric mixer until thick and in soft peaks. Add the caster sugar gradually, whisking well with each addition. The mixture should be glossy and firm. Spoon the meringue over the filling to cover it completely and make a seal with the pastry shell. Swirl the meringue into peaks and sprinkle with the granulated sugar.

5 Bake for 20–30 minutes until the meringue is crispy and pale gold (the centre should still be soft). Allow to cool slightly before serving.

6

TEATIME TREATS

This chapter includes lots of lovely home baking and jam making. It is an area of cooking skills that has never been completely lost despite the fact that fewer of us nowadays have time for tea. This is the sort of cooking that I enjoy enormously and it was my introduction to cooking at a very early age when I was allowed to help with the baking and to make my own little cakes. How many of us remember the thrill of being allowed to scrape the mixing bowl and eat the uncooked cake mixture from the wooden spoon – heaven! There is nothing better than to have the house smelling of delicious baking, whether it is cake-making or bread-baking. Even if you don't have much time to cook generally, a quick batch of scones takes hardly a moment and the results are really wonderful.

I blame Mr Lyons for the decline in baking at home. It was during the 1950s that Joe Lyons opened his chain of tea shops specifically for those women who worked as typists or shop assistants or were just lady shoppers (the forerunners of those 'ladies who lunch') and needed cheap, simple food in clean premises, served quickly. He then started to sell tea, cakes and bread at the cash desk and discovered there was a great demand for them. This led to scientists, not cooks, devising new products, then mass-producing them in a factory – a far cry from domestic baking!

Tea time used to be an important time of the day, a meal to fill the gap before dinner, when bread, butter and cakes were served. At weekends there was always a choice of cakes and also muffins and crumpets. In working-class households, dinner was eaten at lunchtime and tea was a high tea served a little later. It was really an early supper and people ate pies, sausages, ham and even fish and chips, together with bread and butter and perhaps some cake – the whole lot washed down with a good brew of tea.

Coffee mornings eventually seemed to replace tea time. Charity fundraisers would invite people to come for coffee and home-made cakes and biscuits and pay a donation to the charity. Tea time as a daily ritual has almost gone now, apart from when we go out for the day to the countryside or the seaside, when it is usually part of the day out. Cream teas (with clotted cream) in the West Country are a must. Sometimes a trip to town can mean time for tea at a large store after doing a bit of shopping – toasted tea cakes and fancy small cakes are served together with cucumber sandwiches. Taking tea in a large hotel is often a great treat for a birthday or other special occasion.

Jam- and chutney-making has always utilized the excesses of nature. Quite often there is a glut of fruit at certain times of the year and preserving them by jam-making or turning them into chutneys is very satisfying. Although we have a good selection available in the stores, a home-made jam is a special treat and chutney is always a good accompaniment to any cold meat or cheese plate. They also make delightful presents for friends and family.

Tea breads are popular all over the British Isles and there are many of them. They are traditionally made using yeast and are flavoured with fruits and spices. Today, some tea breads are made not with yeast but using bicarbonate of soda or baking powder as a raising agent, but the original recipe using yeast is the best. The Welsh name 'bara brith' means 'speckled bread' and is similar to the Irish barm brack. Serve this in thin slices spread with butter.

WELSH BARA BRITH

Makes 1 loaf

butter, for greasing

175 ml/6 fl oz milk

4 tsp dried yeast

115 g/4 oz brown sugar

450 g/1 lb strong plain flour

½ tsp salt

115 g/4 oz butter

280 g/10 oz mixed dried fruit (sultanas, currants and raisins)

55 g/2 oz mixed peel

1 tsp ground mixed spice

1 egg, beaten

1 Grease a 900-g/2-lb loaf tin.

2 Warm the milk in a saucepan until tepid and add the yeast with 1 teaspoon of the sugar. Mix well and allow to froth in a warm place for 15 minutes.

3 Sift the flour and salt into a mixing bowl. Rub the butter into the flour mixture until it resembles breadcrumbs then add the remaining sugar, dried fruit, peel and mixed spice and stir well. Add the beaten egg and the frothy yeast mixture and mix to form a soft dough.

4 Turn the mixture out onto a floured surface and knead until smooth. Replace the dough in the bowl, cover with clingfilm and place in a warm place to rise for 1–1½ hours until it has doubled in bulk.

5 Preheat the oven to 190°C/375°F/Gas Mark 5.

6 Turn the dough out again and knead lightly. Shape the dough into a rectangle the length of the tin and 3 times the width. Fold the dough into 3 lengthwise and put it in the tin with the join underneath. Cover and leave to rise in a warm place for 30–40 minutes, until it has risen above the tin.

7 Bake towards the bottom of the oven for 30 minutes. Turn the loaf around and cover the top with foil if it is getting too brown. Continue to cook for a further 30 minutes.

8 Turn the loaf out of the tin and tap it on the bottom. If cooked it will sound hollow. If not fully cooked, return it to the oven for a further 10 minutes (without the tin). Leave to cool on a wire rack.

Spices have been used in sweet recipes throughout history and ginger is one of the favourites. A sticky gingerbread is a wonderful cake to serve at tea time, but is also useful for packed lunches, picnics and is traditionally, like its oatmeal cousin Parkin, served on Guy Fawkes Night around the bonfire. Gingerbread includes a lot of sugar, syrup and treacle, which makes it a good keeping cake, and it is worthwhile making a large quantity because it will keep for 2–3 weeks in an airtight tin.

GINGERBREAD

Makes 12–16 pieces

450 g/1 lb plain flour

3 tsp baking powder

1 tsp bicarbonate of soda

3 tsp ground ginger

175 g/6 oz butter

175 g/6 oz soft brown sugar

175 g/6 oz black treacle

175 g/6 oz golden syrup

1 egg, beaten

300 ml/½ pint milk

cream or warmed golden syrup, to serve

1 Line a 23-cm/9-inch square cake tin, 5 cm/2 inches deep, with greaseproof or baking paper.

2 Preheat the oven to 160°C/325°F/Gas Mark 3.

3 Sift the dry ingredients into a large mixing bowl.

4 Place the butter, sugar, treacle and syrup in a medium saucepan and heat over a low heat until the butter has melted and the sugar dissolved. Allow to cool a little.

5 Mix the beaten egg with the milk and add to the cooled syrup mixture.

6 Add all the liquid ingredients to the flour mixture and beat well using a wooden spoon until the mixture is smooth and glossy.

7 Pour the mixture into the prepared tin and bake in the centre of the oven for 1½ hours until well risen and just firm to the touch. A skewer inserted into the cake should come out cleanly if it is cooked. This gives a lovely sticky gingerbread, but if you like a firmer cake cook for a further 15 minutes.

8 Remove from the oven and allow the cake to cool in the tin. When cool, remove the cake from the tin with the lining paper. Over wrap with foil and place in an airtight tin for up to 1 week to allow the flavours to mature.

9 Cut into wedges and serve for tea or serve with cream as a pudding. Extra warmed syrup is an added extravagance.

Bread is the staple food of many countries including Britain. We are lucky to have many good bakers and a wide choice of flours for making our own good-quality, well-flavoured bread, including organic, strong plain white, granary and wholemeal. Bread-making is very simple and therapeutic and there is nothing better to greet your family and guests with than the smell of freshly baked bread in the kitchen. Indeed, nothing makes a house feel more like a home.

FRESH BREAD

Makes 1 large loaf or 8 baps

butter, for greasing

450 g/1 lb strong plain flour

1 tsp salt

1 x 7 g/⅛ oz sachet easy-blend dried yeast

1 tbsp vegetable oil or melted butter

350 ml/12 fl oz tepid water

1 Grease a 900-g/2-lb loaf tin or 2 baking trays.

2 Mix the flour, salt and yeast together in a mixing bowl. Add the oil and water and stir well to form a soft dough.

3 You can use a free-standing electric mixer to knead the dough with the dough hook for 4–5 minutes. Alternatively, turn the dough out onto a lightly floured board and knead well for 5–7 minutes. The dough should have a smooth appearance and feel elastic.

4 Return the dough to the bowl, cover with a cloth or clingfilm and leave in a warm place to rise for about 1 hour until the dough has doubled in size.

5 Turn it out onto a board and knead again until smooth. For a loaf shape, shape as a rectangle the length of the tin and 3 times the width. Fold the dough into 3 and place into the tin with the join underneath so that you have a well-shaped loaf. Alternatively, divide the dough into 8 equal pieces, shape into rounds and space well apart on the baking trays. Dust with a little extra flour for a softer crust. Cover and leave to rise again for about 30 minutes until the loaf is well risen above the tin or the baps are doubled in size.

6 Preheat the oven to 230°C/450°F/Gas Mark 8. If baking a loaf, place the tin in the centre of the oven for 25–30 minutes. If the top is getting too brown, reduce the temperature a little. To test that the loaf is cooked, tip it out of the tin and tap it on the bottom – it should sound hollow. For the baps, bake for 15–20 minutes, swapping the baking trays around half way through the cooking time. Leave to cool on a cooling rack and eat as fresh as possible.

Scones are quick to make and are delicious served freshly baked. Originally from Scotland, scones are now associated with afternoon tea all over Britain, particularly in Devon where the 'cream tea' (scones, jam and clotted cream) is served in all the tea shops. Scones can be made with or without fruit and savoury scones, made with a little grated cheese, are also popular and can be served with various fillings as a good alternative to sandwiches.

SCONES

Makes 10–12

450 g/1 lb plain flour

½ tsp salt

2 tsp baking powder

55 g/2 oz butter

2 tbsp caster sugar

250 ml/9 fl oz milk

3 tbsp milk, for glazing

strawberry jam and clotted cream, to serve

1 Preheat the oven to 220°C/425°F/Gas Mark 7.

2 Sift the flour, salt and baking powder into a bowl. Rub in the butter until the mixture resembles breadcrumbs. Stir in the sugar.

3 Make a well in the centre and pour in the milk. Stir in using a round-bladed knife and make a soft dough.

4 Turn the mixture onto a floured surface and lightly flatten the dough until it is of an even thickness, about 1 cm/½ inch. Don't be heavy-handed, scones need a light touch.

5 Use a 6-cm/2½-inch pastry cutter to cut out the scones and place on the baking tray.

6 Glaze with a little milk and bake for 10–12 minutes, until golden and well risen.

7 Cool on a wire rack and serve freshly baked. Traditionally served with strawberry jam and clotted cream.

VARIATIONS

To make fruit scones, add 55 g/2 oz mixed fruit with the sugar. To make wholemeal scones, use wholemeal flour and omit the sugar. These are delicious to serve with soup or as an accompaniment to cheese. To make cheese scones, omit the sugar and fruit and add 55 g/2 oz finely grated Cheddar or Double Gloucester cheese to the mixture with 1 teaspoon mustard.

Shortbread dates back at least to the sixteenth century, when it was known to be a favourite of Mary Queen of Scots. It is ideal for tea time, coffee in the morning, or as an accompaniment to fruit fools or other soft desserts. The formula for shortbread is one part sugar and two parts butter to three parts flour. The sugar used is usually caster, the butter slightly salted, and the flour plain white, though sometimes a tablespoon of semolina, rice flour or cornflour may replace some of the flour to give a different texture.

SCOTTISH PETTICOAT TAILS SHORTBREAD

Makes 8 pieces

butter, for greasing

175 g/6 oz plain flour, plus 1 tbsp for dusting

pinch of salt

55 g/2 oz caster sugar

115 g/4 oz butter, cut into small pieces

2 tsp golden caster sugar

1 Grease a 20-cm/8-inch fluted cake tin or flan tin.

2 Preheat the oven to 150°C/300°F/Gas Mark 2.

3 Mix together the flour, salt and sugar. Rub the butter into the dry ingredients. Continue to work the mixture until it forms a soft dough. Make sure you do not overwork the shortbread or it will be tough, not crumbly as it should be.

4 Lightly press the dough into the cake tin. If you don't have a fluted tin, roll out the dough on a lightly floured board, place on a baking tray and pinch the edges to form a scalloped pattern.

5 Mark into 8 pieces with a knife. Prick all over with a fork and bake in the centre of the oven for 45–50 minutes until the shortbread is firm and just coloured.

6 Allow to cool in the tin and dredge with the sugar. Cut into portions and remove to a wire rack. Store in an airtight container in a cool place until needed.

Soda bread has been a staple in Ireland for many centuries. It is a bread made without yeast, the raising agent being bicarbonate of soda mixed with buttermilk. It is simple to make, needs very little kneading and no time at all rising. The loaves are cut on the top into a cross shape to help the bread rise and, according to Irish folklore, to let the devils (or the fairies) out. Soda bread can be made with brown or white flour or a mixture of the two and is a wonderful partner for cheese and an ideal accompaniment to soup.

IRISH SODA BREAD

Serves 4–6

450 g/1 lb plain flour

1 tsp salt

1 tsp bicarbonate of soda

400 ml/14 fl oz buttermilk

1 Preheat the oven to 220°C/425°F/Gas Mark 7.

2 Sift the flour, salt and bicarbonate of soda into a mixing bowl.

3 Make a well in the centre of the dry ingredients and pour in most of the buttermilk.

4 Mix well together using your hands. The dough should be very soft but not too wet. If necessary, add the remaining buttermilk.

5 Turn the dough out onto a lightly floured surface and knead it lightly. Shape into a 20-cm/8-inch round.

6 Place the bread on a greased baking tray, cut a cross in the top and bake in the oven for 25–30 minutes. When done it should sound hollow if tapped on the bottom. Eat while still warm. Soda bread is always best eaten the same day as it is made.

VARIATIONS

Add 1 tablespoon chopped fresh rosemary and 55 g/2 oz sultanas. For a change, make with granary flour and add a handful of seeds or coarse oatmeal or make with half stoneground flour and half white flour and 55 g/2 oz chopped walnuts. Sweet soda bread can be made with the addition of 25 g/1 oz sugar and 85 g/3 oz mixed dried fruits. This is known as 'spotted dog'. Another sweet version is made with the addition of 1 tablespoon sugar and 85 g/3 oz roughly chopped chocolate.

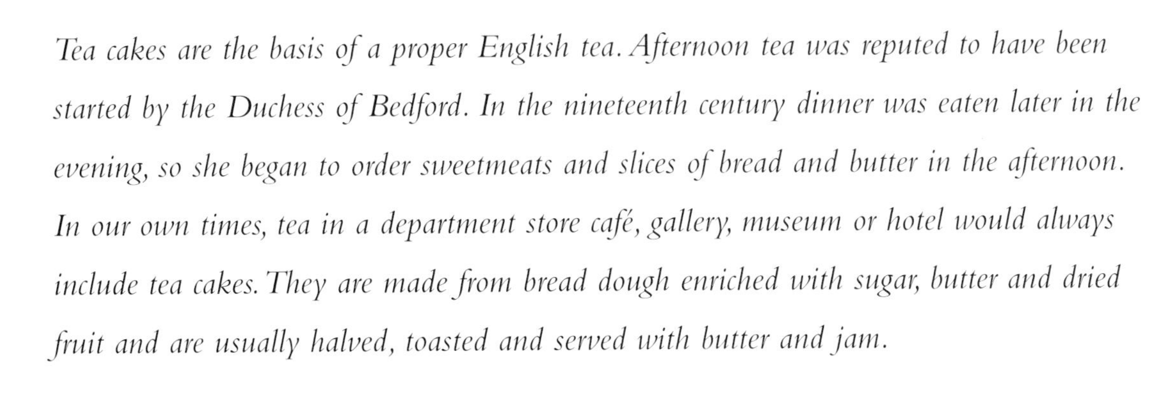

Tea cakes are the basis of a proper English tea. Afternoon tea was reputed to have been started by the Duchess of Bedford. In the nineteenth century dinner was eaten later in the evening, so she began to order sweetmeats and slices of bread and butter in the afternoon. In our own times, tea in a department store café, gallery, museum or hotel would always include tea cakes. They are made from bread dough enriched with sugar, butter and dried fruit and are usually halved, toasted and served with butter and jam.

TEA CAKES

Makes 10–12

300 ml/½ pint milk

4 tsp dried yeast

55 g/2 oz caster sugar

450 g/1 lb strong plain flour

1 tsp salt

1 tsp ground mixed spice

115 g/4 oz currants

25 g/1 oz mixed peel, chopped

55 g/2 oz butter, melted

1 egg, beaten

sugar glaze made from 2 tbsp sugar and 2 tbsp warm milk

1 Warm the milk in a saucepan until just tepid and add the yeast with 1 teaspoon of the sugar. Mix well and allow to froth in a warm place for 15 minutes.

2 Sift the flour, salt and spice into a large mixing bowl and add the currants, peel and the remaining sugar.

3 Make a well in the centre of the dry ingredients and pour in the milk mixture, the melted butter and egg.

4 Mix well using a wooden spoon at first and then by hand.

5 Turn out onto a lightly floured surface and knead lightly until the dough is smooth and elastic.

6 Put the dough back into the bowl, cover with clingfilm and leave to rise in a warm place for 40–45 minutes until it has doubled in size.

7 Knead the dough again lightly and divide into 10–12 even-sized buns, shaping well.

8 Preheat the oven to 220°C/425°F/Gas Mark 7.

9 Place the buns on two greased baking trays, cover with a damp tea towel or large plastic bags and allow to rise again for 30–40 minutes.

10 Bake the tea cakes in the oven for 18–20 minutes until they are golden brown. Remove from the oven, place on a wire rack and glaze with the sugar glaze while still hot.

Eccles cakes come from the small town of Eccles near Manchester. They were devised by the niece of Elizabeth Raffald, who was a well-known cook in the area. Being a Lancastrian, these are the first sort of cakes I was allowed to make. My aunt would do all her baking on a certain day and at the end of the session, I would be able to make Eccles cakes with her leftover flaky or puff pastry. The filling would be any leftover fruit mixed with butter and brown sugar and sometimes some spices.

ECCLES CAKES

Makes 10–12

400 g/14 oz ready-made puff pastry
2 tbsp plain flour, for dusting
55 g/2 oz butter, softened
55 g/2 oz soft brown sugar
85 g/3 oz currants
25 g/1 oz mixed peel, chopped
½ tsp ground mixed spice (optional)
1 egg white, lightly beaten
1 tsp caster sugar

1 Preheat the oven to 220°C/425°F/Gas Mark 7.

2 Roll out the pastry thinly, using the flour to dust the work surface and the rolling pin.

3 Cut into rounds using a 9-cm/3½-inch cutter. Fold the trimmings carefully, re-roll and repeat the cuttings to give a total of 10–12 rounds.

4 In a basin, mix together the butter and soft brown sugar until creamy, then add the dried fruit and mixed spice, if using.

5 Put a teaspoon of the filling in the centre of each pastry round. Draw the edges of the circles together and pinch the edges over the filling. Reshape each cake into a round.

6 Turn the cakes over and lightly roll them with the rolling pin until the currants just show through. Score with a knife into a lattice pattern.

7 Place the cakes on a greased baking tray and allow to rest for 10–15 minutes.

8 Brush the cakes with the egg white, sprinkle with the caster sugar and bake at the top of the oven for about 15 minutes until golden brown and crisp.

9 Transfer to a wire rack and sprinkle with a little more sugar if desired. Delicious straight from the oven, they also keep well in an airtight tin for a week and can be reheated before serving.

English muffins are somewhat reminiscent of Dickens novels: cold winter snow scenes and roaring log fires spied through a frosty window. Muffins go back a long way and were sold hot on the streets of London in the nineteenth century. The English muffin is a light, yeast-based, enriched bread, which is cooked on a griddle to give a crunchy top and bottom with a soft inside. They should be split while hot, a piece of butter placed in the centre and pressed back together again before eating immediately.

ENGLISH MUFFINS

Makes 10–12

- 2 x 7 g/⅛ oz sachets easy-blend dried yeast
- 250 ml/9 fl oz tepid water
- 125 ml/4 fl oz natural yogurt
- 450 g/1 lb strong plain flour
- ½ tsp salt
- 50 g/1¾ oz fine semolina
- oil, for greasing

to serve

- butter
- jam (optional)

1 Mix the yeast with half the tepid water in a bowl until it has dissolved.

2 Add the remaining water and the yogurt and mix well.

3 Sieve the flour into a large bowl and add the salt. Pour in the yeast liquid and mix well to a soft dough.

4 Turn out onto a floured surface and knead well until very smooth. Put the dough back into the bowl, cover with clingfilm and leave to rise for 30–40 minutes in a warm place until it has doubled in size.

5 Turn out again onto the surface and knead lightly. Roll out the dough to a thickness of 2 cm/¾ inch.

6 Using a 7.5-cm/3-inch cutter, cut into rounds and scatter the semolina over each muffin. Re-roll the trimmings of the dough and make further muffins until it is all used up. Place them on a lightly floured baking tray, cover and allow to rise again for 30–40 minutes.

7 Heat a griddle or a large frying pan and lightly grease with a little oil. Cook half the muffins for 7–8 minutes on each side, taking care not to burn them. Repeat with the rest of the muffins.

8 Serve freshly cooked with lots of butter. Muffins can be kept for 2 days in an airtight tin. To reheat, split them across the centre and quickly toast them before serving with butter and jam.

It is said that this was the favourite cake of Queen Victoria. It is sometimes called a sponge cake, but a sponge contains no fat and one of the most important ingredients of this cake is good butter. The cake is traditionally made by the creaming method, although today you can easily make it by the all-in-one method – just make sure the butter is softened, add 1 teaspoon of baking powder to the flour and then beat all the ingredients together with an electric mixer. It makes a useful base for a child's birthday cake.

VICTORIA SANDWICH CAKE

Makes 8–10 slices

175 g/6 oz butter, at room temperature

175 g/6 oz caster sugar

3 eggs, beaten

175 g/6 oz self-raising flour

pinch of salt

to serve

3 tbsp raspberry jam

1 tbsp caster or icing sugar

1 Preheat the oven to 180°C/350°F/Gas Mark 4.

2 Grease 2 x 20-cm/8-inch sponge tins and base-line with greaseproof paper or baking paper.

3 Cream the butter and sugar together in a mixing bowl using a wooden spoon or a hand-held mixer until the mixture is pale in colour and light and fluffy.

4 Add the egg a little at a time, beating well after each addition.

5 Sift the flour and salt and carefully add to the mixture, folding it in with a metal spoon or a spatula.

6 Divide the mixture between the tins and smooth over with the spatula.

7 Place them on the same shelf in the centre of the oven and bake for 25–30 minutes until well risen, golden brown and beginning to shrink from the sides of the tin.

8 Remove from the oven and allow to stand for 1 minute.

9 Loosen the cakes from around the edge of the tins using a palette knife. Turn the cakes out onto a clean tea towel, remove the paper and invert them onto a wire rack (this prevents the wire rack from marking the top of the cakes).

10 When completely cool, sandwich together with the jam and sprinkle with the sugar. The cake is delicious when freshly baked, but any remaining cake can be stored in an airtight tin for up to 1 week.

Toast is a great snack, whether buttered hot or topped with Marmite, honey or jam, and something on toast is always a good tea-time treat. The simplest is obviously beans, but some old favourites like Welsh rarebit remain very popular. There were English, Scottish and Welsh varieties as early as the eighteenth century, but the Welsh version is the one that seems to have lasted longest. Traditionally it was made with Welsh cheese, but it is now made with any well-flavoured Cheddar.

WELSH RAREBIT

Serves 4

4 slices of bread

225 g/8 oz mature Cheddar cheese, grated

25 g/1 oz butter

3 tbsp beer

salt and pepper

½ tsp dry mustard powder

1 egg, beaten

1 Toast the bread under a medium grill on 1 side only.

2 Put the cheese into a saucepan and add the butter and beer. Heat slowly over a low heat, stirring continuously. Add some salt and pepper and the mustard powder and stir well until the mixture is thick and creamy. Allow to cool slightly before adding the egg.

3 Spread the rarebit over the untoasted side of the bread and place under the hot grill until golden and bubbling. Serve at once.

VARIATIONS

Scotch Woodcock

Toast 4 slices of granary or oat bread on both sides. Butter the slices and divide 12 anchovy fillets among them, keeping them warm. Melt 25 g/1 oz butter in a saucepan, add 6 beaten eggs and 2 tablespoons double cream. Season with salt, pepper and a pinch of cayenne pepper. Stir over a low heat, until the eggs are softly scrambled but still moist. Spoon the eggs over the anchovy toasts and serve with a sprinkling of snipped fresh chives. Serves 4.

Stilton Toasties

Toast 4 slices of bread, ideally onion or walnut bread. Spread each slice with a tablespoon of chutney or a good teaspoon of whole-grain mustard and top with 175 g/6 oz crumbled Stilton cheese. Place under a hot grill and grill until the cheese is softened and slightly browning. Serve at once. Serves 4.

Crumpets have always been associated with winter firesides and tea time and there is nothing nicer than to sit by a roaring fire with a toasting fork in your hand toasting crumpets. Spreading them with lots of butter until it drips through your fingers is also part of enjoying crumpets. In some parts of England and in Wales they are better known as pikelets. Crumpets are now readily available, but to make them at home is a magical experience as the traditional 'bubble' appearance develops.

CRUMPETS

Makes 10–12

350 g/12 oz plain flour

pinch of salt

15 g/½ oz fresh yeast

1 tsp caster sugar

400 ml/14 fl oz tepid milk

butter, to serve

1 Place the flour and salt in a mixing bowl and mix together. Blend the fresh yeast with the sugar in a basin and add the milk.

2 Pour the liquid onto the flour and mix everything together until the batter is smooth, beating the batter thoroughly so that it is light and airy. Cover and leave to rise in a warm place for 1 hour until well risen.

3 Stir the batter to knock out any air and check the consistency. If it is too thick, add 1 tablespoon of water (it should look rather gloopy). Leave aside for 10 minutes.

4 Grease the frying pan and 4 crumpet rings or 7.5-cm/3-inch plain cutters. Place the frying pan over a medium heat and leave to heat up for 2 minutes. Arrange the rings in the pan and spoon in enough batter to come halfway up each ring. Cook over a low heat for 5–6 minutes until small holes begin to appear and the top is starting to dry.

5 Remove the crumpet rings with a palette knife or an oven glove. Turn the crumpets over (the base should be golden brown) and cook the top for just 1–2 minutes to cook through.

6 Keep the first batch of crumpets warm while you cook the rest of the batter.

7 Serve freshly cooked with butter or if you want to serve them later, allow them to cool and reheat in a toaster or by the fire.

In Britain pancakes are always associated with Shrove Tuesday, or 'Pancake Day', when we are meant to use up any rich foods, particularly eggs, which we should not be eating during Lent. In other countries the day is known as 'Mardi gras' or 'Fat Tuesday'. It is a custom in Britain to hold pancake races with people tossing pancakes as they run. Pancakes are wonderfully versatile and can be served simply with sugar and lemon juice, with ice cream, fruit or chocolate sauce, or stuffed with meat, cheese or vegetables.

PANCAKES

Makes 10

100 g/3½ oz plain flour

pinch of salt

1 egg, beaten

300 ml/½ pint milk

10 tsp butter (for sweet pancakes) or oil (for savoury ones)

to serve

lemon wedges

caster sugar

warmed honey or jam

1 Place the flour and salt in a mixing bowl. Make a well in the centre and add the egg and half the milk. Using a whisk, beat the egg and milk together and gradually incorporate the flour. Continue beating until the mixture is smooth and there are no lumps. Gradually beat in the remaining milk. Pour the batter mixture into a jug and set aside for 30 minutes.

2 Heat an 18-cm/7-inch frying pan over a medium heat and add 1 teaspoon of the butter or oil, depending on what you are going to eat with the pancakes.

3 Pour in enough batter to just cover the base and swirl the batter around the frying pan while tilting it so that you have a thin even layer. Cook for about 30 seconds and then lift up the edge of the pancake and see if it is brown. Loosen the pancake around the edges and flip it over with a spatula or palette knife. Alternatively, have a go at tossing the pancakes by flipping the pan quickly with a deft flick of the wrist and catching it carefully.

4 Cook on the other side until golden brown and then turn out onto a warm plate, cover with foil and keep warm while you cook all the pancakes in the remaining butter or oil. Layer them with baking paper so you can separate them at the end.

5 Serve them with lemon and sugar, warmed honey or jam, or a filling of your choice.

Jam making at home is sadly a dying art. Just try making a small quantity and you will be surprised how easy it is and what a superior product you can achieve. Strawberry jam is probably Britain's favourite, but it is a little difficult to make satisfactorily because strawberries don't contain enough pectin to make a firm set. A simpler one to make is raspberry because it sets easily. Use it on scones or hot buttered toast, but also to fill a Victoria sandwich cake, in a trifle and as a sauce over ice cream.

RASPBERRY JAM

Makes 5 x 450 g/1 lb jars

1.3 kg/3 lb raspberries

1.3 kg/3 lb granulated or preserving sugar

1 You will need 5 x 450 g/1 lb jam jars with lids and waxed discs. To sterilize the jars, make sure they are washed in soapy water and rinsed well and then heat in a moderate oven for 5 minutes.

2 Put the fruit into a large saucepan and slowly cook until some of the juices begin to run. Simmer gently for 15–20 minutes until tender. Add the sugar and stir until dissolved.

3 Raise the heat and boil hard for 2–3 minutes until setting point is reached. Test if it is set by using a sugar thermometer. When it reads 105°C/221°F it is at a good setting point. Alternatively, test by dropping a small spoonful of jam onto a cold saucer, refrigerate to cool, then push it with a clean finger. If it forms a wrinkled skin it is ready. If not, boil for 1 further minute and repeat.

4 Remove the pan from the heat and allow to cool for 2 minutes, skimming if necessary.

5 Have the jars warmed in a moderate oven and fill carefully using a ladle and a jam funnel. Top with the waxed discs and screw on the lids. Wipe the jars clean and leave to cool. Label and date to avoid confusion later.

6 Store in a cool, dry place. Once opened the jam will keep for up to 2 months in the refrigerator.

Lemon curd is a delicious preserve that is useful to make during the spring months when there is no particular fruit in season. It is easy to make and best eaten fresh, but it can be stored for up to 2 months in the refrigerator. Orange curd can also be made using Seville oranges when in season (January and February) and a lime curd can be made for those who prefer a slightly sharper spread. Use on buttered scones and crumpets, to sandwich together a Victoria sandwich cake or to make luscious lemon tarts.

LEMON CURD

Makes 700 g/1 lb 9 oz

- 3 unwaxed lemons
- 350 g/12 oz caster sugar
- 3 eggs, beaten
- 175 g/6 oz butter

1 You will need 2 jam jars or 3–4 small jars with lids and waxed discs. To sterilize the jars, make sure they are washed in soapy water and rinsed well and then heat in a moderate oven for 5 minutes.

2 Carefully grate the rind from each of the lemons using a fine grater. Make sure you only take the yellow rind and not the bitter white pith.

3 Cut the lemons in half and squeeze out all the juice, then sieve to remove the pips.

4 Place a medium heatproof bowl over a saucepan of simmering water and add the lemon rind, juice and sugar. Mix together well until the sugar has dissolved.

5 Add the eggs and the butter cut into small pieces and continue to stir for 25–30 minutes until the butter has melted and the mixture begins to thicken. Beat well and turn into the jars. Cover and label before storing. Once opened the lemon curd will keep for up to 2 months in the refrigerator.

VARIATIONS

To make orange curd, use 3 Seville oranges instead of the lemons, and for lime prepare 5 limes for the same amount of the other ingredients. Blackberries and blackcurrants can also be made into curd by stewing the fruit first and sieving to make a purée.

Making chutneys from fruits and vegetables when there is a glut can be very rewarding and they have re-emerged as a fashionable food served in many restaurants to accompany hot and cold meats. A good home-made chutney is a real asset to any table. Onion marmalade is one particular British favourite, tomato chutney has always been popular, and pickled vegetables such as piccalilli are also enjoying a renaissance. The simplest of all chutneys is apple.

APPLE CHUTNEY

Makes 4 x 450 g/1 lb jars

1.3 kg/3 lb cooking apples, peeled, cored and diced into 1-cm/½-inch cubes

900 g/2 lb onions, finely chopped

2–3 garlic cloves, crushed

600 ml/1 pint distilled spice vinegar

450 g/1 lb raisins

700 g/1 lb 9 oz soft brown sugar

2 tsp ground ginger

2 tsp ground mixed spice

½ tsp paprika

1 tsp salt

1 You will need 4 x 450 g/1 lb jam jars with lids and waxed discs. To sterilize the jars, make sure they are washed in soapy water and rinsed well and then heat in a moderate oven for 5 minutes.

2 Place the apples into a large saucepan with the onion, garlic and vinegar. Bring to the boil and cook gently for up to 1 hour until the fruit and onion are thick and pulpy.

3 Add the raisins, sugar, spices and salt. Bring back to a simmer and cook for a further 20 minutes until a good consistency is achieved. The liquid should have all been absorbed but the chutney should still be moist and not at all dry.

4 Have the jars warmed in a moderate oven and fill carefully using a ladle and a jam funnel while the chutney is still hot. Top with the waxed discs and cover with a layer of cellophane to prevent the lids corroding. Screw on the lids. Wipe the jars clean and leave to cool. Label and date.

5 This chutney is better if it is stored for at least 1 week before use to develop its flavour. Store in a cool, dry, dark place. Once opened the apple chutney will keep for up to 2 months in the refrigerator.

This fresh fruit drink, which can easily be made at home, is far more delicious than many of today's fizzy soft drinks and contains a lot less sugar and no artificial preservatives or flavourings. Real lemonade is also a real thirst quencher and a great favourite with both the young and old. This recipe is for the traditional still version, but a fizzy lemonade can be made by diluting the lemon syrup with some sparkling mineral or soda water (see Variations).

LEMONADE

Makes about 1.2 litres/2 pints

3 unwaxed lemons

200 g/7 oz caster sugar

1 litre/1¾ pints boiling water

to serve

ice cubes

strips of lemon rind

1 Wash the lemons and grate the rind with a fine grater, taking care just to remove the yellow rind and leave the bitter white pith behind. Alternatively, remove the rind in long stips using a potato peeler.

2 Place the rind and sugar in a measuring jug and pour over the boiling water. Stir well until the sugar is dissolved, cover and leave to cool.

3 Halve the lemons, squeeze out the juice and add to the jug.

4 Strain the lemonade through a fine sieve or muslin. Serve chilled with ice and a strip of lemon rind. This lemonade keeps in the refrigerator for 4–5 days.

VARIATIONS

Quick Lemonade

Chop up 3 whole lemons and place in a liquidizer with 200 g/7 oz caster sugar and 1 litre/1¾ pints cold water. Blitz for 30 seconds and strain through a fine sieve. If the lemon flavour is too intense, add more sugar. Serve at once.

Lemon Syrup

Put the rind of 2 lemons in a saucepan, add 450 g/1 lb sugar and 300 ml/½ pint water and heat until the sugar has dissolved, bring to the boil and heat for 2–3 minutes. Allow to cool and then add 300 ml/½ pint lemon juice, strain into a jug and pour into sterilized bottles. The syrup keeps in the refrigerator for up to 1 week. Dilute to taste with sparkling water or soda water and serve at once.

Before the advent of canned soft drinks, people made their own fizzy drinks at home. To put in the 'fizz', they used yeast, which gives off the carbon dioxide needed to add bubbles to the drink. Home-made ginger beer was very popular and is a lot of fun to make. It involves creating a 'ginger beer plant' first, using yeast, then feeding the plant for 10 days before making the ginger beer. Store in a cool place because it is essential that the beer remains cool and ensure that your bottles have tight-fitting stoppers.

GINGER BEER

Makes about 4.5 litres/8 pints

500 g/1 lb 2 oz caster sugar

4.2 litres/7½ pints water

juice of 2 lemons

for the 'plant'

55 g/2 oz fresh yeast

25 g/1 oz caster sugar, plus extra for fermenting

25 g/1 oz ground ginger, plus extra for fermenting

300 ml/½ pint water

1 You will need 8 x 600 ml/1 pint screw-topped or old-fashioned (with metal and rubber fasteners) beer bottles and a piece of fine muslin. To sterilize the bottles, wash thoroughly and place in a large saucepan, cover with cold water and bring to the boil. Boil for 5 minutes before removing and drain before use.

2 To make the 'plant', in a bowl blend the yeast with the sugar until creamy, then mix in the ginger. Add the water and stir until well mixed.

3 Place the mixture in a large jar with a loose-fitting lid and store in a cool place for 10 days. Every day you need to add 1 teaspoon each of sugar and ginger and stir well, then re-cover and leave.

4 At the end of 10 days, dissolve the caster sugar in a saucepan with 850 ml/ 1½ pints of the water. Bring to the boil and allow to cool slightly. Sieve the lemon juice and add to the pan.

5 Strain the 'plant' through a fine muslin and add to the sugar and lemon juice in the saucepan. Add the remaining water and stir well.

6 Bottle at once and store in a cool place. Check from time to time as sometimes the bottles blow their tops. Keep for a few days before drinking. The ginger beer will keep unopened for 1–2 months.

7 Serve chilled in tall glasses for a wonderful thirst quencher on a hot summer's day.

INDEX